The Jedi Acade

The Jedi Circle:

Jedi Philosophy for Everyday Life.

THE JEDI CIRCLE
Jedi Philosophy for Everyday Life.

K.S. Trout
The Jedi Academy Online

jediacademyonline.com
Valencia, California

<u>This Book is Dedicated to</u> Carolyn and Dennis – without your continual support this would not be possible. To Jaden – you have been my inspirational Jiminy Cricket. It is my goal to make sure this is the first of many dedications to all of you.

Publisher: CreateSpace.com and Amazon.com
The Jedi Academy Online
Valencia CA. 91354
USA
Telephone Number: (On Request)
Web Site: http://jediacademyonline.com
E-Mail: admin@jediacademyonline.com
Copyright © 2012 The Jedi Academy Online

Acknowledgments, References, and Disclaimers:
Trinity University and the Library (Cover Image).
George Lucas and Lucasfilms LTD. - All Star Wars related material Copyright and Trademark of Lucasfilms LTD. All Rights Reserved.
Disney and all related Copyrights and trademarks – All Rights Reserved.
Power of the Jedi Sourcebook – Copyright 2002 Lucasfilms LTD. All Rights Reserved.
Star Wars Roleplaying Guide 2nd Edition – Copyright 1996 Lucasfilms LTD. All Rights Reserved.
Jedi Apprentice Series - Jude Watson. Copyright Lucasfilms LTD. All Rights Reserved.
Star Wars and all related material used without permission for educational purposes only.
Jedi Academy Online – Copyright 2007-2012
I'd like to give Special Thanks to: Carolyn and Dennis, Jedi Community as a whole; including the following websites: Jedi Academy online, Jedi Temple, JEDI.org, Real Jedi Knights, and Tenebrae Surgunt. Individually I'd like to also include Jaden (HT), Joshua G., Tercenya, Seasin Abrea, Sirius Unduli, Silver, Relan Volkum, Morken Saan, Tionne, Chris-Tien Jinn, Arkai Halon, Steffan Karrde, Streen, and Mindas Ar'ran.

Author: K.S. Trout
Title: The Jedi Circle: Jedi Philosophy for Everyday Life.
ISBN-13: 978-1482637427
ISBN-10: 1482637421

Editor: Opie Macleod.
Cover Design: Opie Macleod © 2012
Page Design: Opie Macleod © 2012
Printed and Bound: CreateSpace and Amazon.com

CONTENTS

::INTRODUCTION::

FAIR WARNING

Before we begin I wanted to clear up a few things. First off, online I use the name Opie Macleod. Kevin Trout, K.S. Trout, Opie Macleod, all names which I have used. The reason for this mixture of names is relatively simple. When I first joined the online Jedi Community you simply did not use your real name online. There was no myspace, facebook, or linkedin. You sought to protect your identity and chose a screen name. For me that was a combination of my offline nickname and last name of my favorite tv series at the time (Highlander). It was been over 16 years since I created that online name. It has earned a reputation and has come to mean something. It is recognized within the Jedi Community. As such I continue to use it. However when writing these books I wanted to use and publish under my real name. Originally I sought to be all author-y with the abbreviations. After a couple of interviews I chose simply to use my name as is. This is why there can be some confusion on Kevin Trout and Opie Macleod.

Second thing I wish to offer is a warning. I am not a professional writer. Meaning I did not go to school for it. I did not major in it. I have never taken any writing classes or seminars. My typing skills are not great. My command of the English language is worse. There will be mistakes throughout this book. Grammar mistakes, misplaced words, typos, etc. I offer my apologies in advance for this. I do this for every book I write. It is my hope that the more I write the better I get at correcting these issues. Time shall tell if that turns out to be true.

Third thing is that this is a second edition. I have added and changed this book a bit. This is an improved version. Yes that paragraph above still applies. I apologize to previous owners, but hope new readers will enjoy the added content and cleaner read.

MY JOURNEY

I find it hard to offer a beginning that does not start either in the middle of my life or the origins of humankind. As such the prelude may be a bit longer than I would like, yet just as important. With that in mind I ask that you bear with me as I seek to get to the beginning. You see, I am a member of Generation X. And as such I grew up with a generation of Parents who saw Buck Rogers, Captain Kirk, and Luke Skywalker and thought why not? Hand-held communication devices? Why not? Space Travel, why not? It has been the history of humans to question why not and achieve great things. From Submarines to Airplanes our imaginations created it first and then someone came along and asked why we couldn't do it. Given answers in the form of problems, they found ways to solve them.

Continuing in that tradition, our generation saw cellphones and asked why they had to be the size of our heads. Given the problems of why, we set out and solved them. Now we have doors that open on their own, world news in the palm of your hand, instant communication almost anywhere in the world. The human imagination has run wild for years and now what we considered Science Fiction is simply Science. We have not stopped, we keep progressing and even our minds are being changed in a better direction. How can this advancements help our world? How can we use these gifts for the betterment of all? While we still have a long way to go, we can see the beginning of a future worth fighting for.

This is the vision I grew up with. These are the things I saw as a child. I saw those before me looking at the impossible, saying why not to a problem and solving it. My problems however were much more personal. While I was awed by Star Trek: The Next Generation just as my Father was awed by the original, I was inspired not to solve technological problems, but personal problems. As young as I was, I still had let people down, I had not been brave enough, or strong enough, or smart enough to be of help. As such people suffered while I hated myself for not being more useful or capable.

So when I saw my heroes being challenged and facing those challenges I thought, why not? Why can't I do the same thing. As fate would have it, or whatever you wish to call coincidence, this came to me while watching Star Wars: The Empire Strikes Back on VHS. As I was listening to Yoda teaching young Skywalker, I could not help but think why couldn't I be Luke Skywalker? Why couldn't I be better than him? That little green muppet had a point, he made sense, and it seemed that this piece of fiction could actually have something.

So, like many inspired by that old space saga, I began my Jedi training in the backyard with a stick. I ran, I jumped, I sat quietly, I observed life around me. I sought to avoid anger, fear, and aggression, for those were the Dark Side. But being a teenager rarely fosters calmness, peace, and patience. However it did offer many learning experiences, real world reality checks for being a Jedi in something closer to Mos Eisley Cantina than in a swamp hut all by one's self. Growing up in the Los Angeles area definitely imparted a few life lessons, especially in regards to a Jedi's diplomacy.

But it all seemed like a personal quest. My own journey to become a real life Jedi. Of course more than once it simply seemed like a silly dream from a kid refusing to grow up. As such I sough real world answers. I looked into various religions such as Christianity and Buddhism. I looked into Eastern Philosophies such as Confucianism and Taoism. Western Philosophies and ideals such as Altruism and Stoicism. I looked into Self-Defense, started where all fan boys start, Bruce Lee. That is just the tip of the iceberg of Martial Arts of course and the flood gates had been opened. When I found myself in College I majored in Philosophy. After college I moved to meet more who were like me, who carried the Jedi name. But I am getting ahead of myself.

See during this time I had made a pretty interesting discovery. With the re-release of the Star Wars Trilogy in 1997 and that generation I was talking about earlier making leaps and

3

bounds in technology two things came together. The Internet and Star Wars fans; these two have a long history. Probably more than I'll ever know. However it was around this time that I also enjoyed the rest and slowly started to populate the world wide web. It wasn't until 1999 that I had found a home online, a place where many like myself could be found. People who were seeking to better themselves, for whatever reason, and they had found the ideal of self-betterment within the Jedi of Star Wars.

We discussed the Jedi Code as written in the Star Wars role-playing guide by West End games. We discussed Yoda and Obi-Wan quotes about the Force. And the few who had studied other philosophies and religions wowed us with the subjects George Lucas drew from. We were the picture definition of geeks and nerds. So busy discussing the ideals online that we rarely got around to doing what needed to be done offline. You know, like actually trying to live as Jedi.

I know how silly it sounds to say I am a Jedi. But it is still there, that core question. "I am a Jedi." "You can't be." Why not? A Jedi is defined by actions, by guidelines. All paths have a beginning and while I certainly cannot lift a car out of the mud. What I can do is be in shape and push that car out of the mud. I may not be able to wield a lightsaber (because obviously they do not exist), but I can study self-defense and defend myself if attacked. I may not wear Jedi Robes, but I can wear nice clothes in warm earth tones (brown slacks, tan shirt, etc.). I may not be able to defend the galaxy from Sith Lords, but I can become a Police Officer to protect and serve peace and justice in my local area. These are just rough examples.

I can live by the philosophy of the Jedi. This means I live my life in accordance to the Jedi Path. Peace over Emotions, Knowledge over Ignorance, Serenity over Passions, Harmony over Chaos, and the Force in the face of Death. The Jedi Path is not my religion, it does not and will not answer the questions about the after-life, the creation of the universe, or if there is some all powerful deity. The Force is energy and energy that is a part of all of us, it is in the world all around us.

This is what I found and this is what I ask "why not" too. The Jedi Path is a lifestyle based upon the works of George Lucas and many other contributors that work for LucasArts and LucasFilms LTD (and soon Disney). It is Science Fiction, but there are many things, many aspects which simply are Science. As our technology grows, so should we grow as human beings. The Jedi Path is one of many great paths in life in which to enrich yourself and experience personal growth.

Throughout my life as I sought to make the Jedi a reality, I met some great people. Experience some great things. It has been an adventure when I wasn't even looking for one. Sure my story is not as exciting as Luke Skywalker or tragic as Obi-Wan Kenobi's. But there were moments which really made me realize the beauty and reality of the Path of a Jedi. And my journey is far form over, at least I hope it is far from over. There is still plenty to do. Both in my own personal growth as a Jedi and for the Jedi Path as a whole.

There are many hurdles out there. Jediism right now with the publicity of people who pray to Yoda or people who refuse to take off their hood. As if that is some sort of Jedi belief or law. And even worse seeking to sue and harass companies and individuals who requested that the said "Jedi" respect the policies/rules of the establishments they were in. This is a prime example of what a Jedi is not, and why in the early days we should have been more focused on the reality of our path. These individuals set the Jedi Path back, placing us right back with the Star Wars fans.

While I am still a fan of Star Wars, the Jedi have grown much further. We have our own systems and techniques. Our own philosophies, and guidelines. We have lessons and lectures to help individuals follow that dream and become a Jedi Knight within today's society. And while it certainly is not as cool or as glamorous as the fictional Jedi, we are carving out the beginning. Who knows where that will lead us. Maybe in 300 years from now, there will be a Order of individuals who wear hooded robes and wield swords of light who stand to protect the innocent and defend peace and justice in the galaxy (or even just Earth). Who can say for sure. What we can say is, why not strive for it? If we do not live it, if we do not pursue it, we will never know for sure. We must be willing to chase our dreams, but more than that we must we willing to fail at them. You cannot allow the fear of failure hold you back. You have to be willing to give 100% in order to make your dream come true. If you do not, at least you know you left everything out there. There won't be a question of, "if I had just tried harder." Because you will know you gave it your all and there were only two options available to you. Fail or succeed. For me, for the Jedi, the verdict is still out, but certainly we are making a strong case for success.

JEDI: THE OVERVIEW

I would just like to offer a small overview of the Jedi Path in general. After all if this is your first introduction into the actual Jedi Philosophy than you probably have a lot of questions which will not be answered by Jedi Theory. So I want to just talk about the Jedi Path in general a bit and help pass some understanding about what we do. As well as note why this isn't s crazy as it first sounds.

Peace of mind, calm spirit, patience, discipline, responsibility, courage. These are traits that each of us wouldn't mind having a bit more of. And while we see many books and groups offering this we still wonder if it can be for real. Who can they point to as an example and say "See? That is the goal, that is what you can become." We have that inspiration, that icon, that goal of peace, calmness, strength, and wisdom. Jedi Knights. A symbol of all that and more. But how can we be like them? They are fiction and we are stuck in the rat-race of society.

Jedi Philosophy is a concept born of fiction and turned into reality. It is something a Jedi lives in their daily lives. No temples, no lightsabers, no robes, just everyday people living their lives in accordance with Jedi ideals and practices. Sure Star Wars is fiction, there is no denying that. Yet authors and creators drew inspiration from many real world sources to build that fictional order of mystical knights. They did such a great job that there is no one real world comparison. There is not a single path out there that is exactly like the Jedi Knights.

Taoism, Christianity, Zen Buddhism, Stoicism, many beliefs and ideals we can look at which carry similarities. Yet they also carry differences. So those inspired by Star Wars, those who saw the Jedi Knights and felt they were worth aspiring too took it upon themselves to make the Jedi Path a reality. In the beginning these Jedi borrowed from a lot of preexisting paths to help fill the gaps. However, as the years rolled by and the Jedi began to gain real world experience living as Jedi in their daily lives, they also began to develop their own methods and practices.

In late 1998 I joined the online Jedi Community which was just forming up. The re-release of the Star Wars movies plus the anticipation of the new prequels along with the emerging ease of communication provided by the internet started a movement. It sparked an idea and a question began to form – Why Not? Why can't we be Jedi? Why can we take the philosophy and live by it in our lives? Over the next 13 years we attacked those questions. We hit road blocks, we found problems, and we fell on our faces more than once. Yet we didn't stop, we learned from each failure, we grew and progressed with one another and have stopped yet.

In this time I developed a text to help simplify and condense the Jedi Ideals into an easy to follow guide. I originally called it, the Circle of the Jedi. Due to the format (five by five) and my enjoyment of Ba-Gua at the time. My roomate and dear friend at the time Mindas Ar'ran helped me as I formed this idea into something practical and useful. Something which could be applied to daily life for those aspiring to be Jedi. In 2005 I released to the greater Jedi Community to seek their thoughts. The Circle of the Jedi evolved and became the Jedi Circle. Some aspects were changed, semantic issues were addressed. The overall layout was kept the same, yet certain elements were replaced. In traits Strong/Strength was replaced with Reliability. Observation was replaced due to already having Awareness in the practices. These examples mark the growth the Circle went through in its continual development.

So as one might imagine, this is a guide to living like a Jedi in our everyday life. Attaining that peace of mind even in the middle of a busy fast food restaurant; whether you are working or a customer. Having patience when sitting in your car during a traffic jam. Having clear, calm, logical points when debating and having discussions on the most heated topics. These things are not out of our reach. It is merely that we rarely find people that teach and support us in reaching them. For us we find that the symbol is there, albeit fiction it is still something we can aspire to.

Something we can live every single day; being a Jedi Knight.

JEDI AS A PHILOSOPHY?

The Jedi Philosophy has been debated for years and many people still do not have a clear idea about the philosophical ideology of the Jedi as represented by people today. George Lucas was inspired by many things when he created Star Wars. While he has been quoted as to what he drew his inspiration from, that does not define the Jedi philosophy itself. Jedi are not Samurai, they are not solely based on Stoicism or Altruism, and they are not merely Arthurian Knights. Nor are Jedi simply following Joseph Campbell's Hero's Journey. The Jedi can be linked and compared to many things because they share many common ideals and practices. But this does not mean they are the same as those other beliefs.

This book will show two things by the end. The first being that the Jedi have their own philosophy, their own path in life. Indeed we have similarities, yet we are in fact our own organization. The second is that while the Jedi draw their inspiration from Star Wars they are not crazed fans who cannot tell reality from fiction. Instead the Jedi have over the years developed a solid philosophical path that can be followed daily. The Jedi Path is an actuality, not a dream, not a science fiction novel, but something born from inspiration and grounded in reality.

This book will guide one through the Jedi Circle, one of the core non-fictional sources of Jedi Philosophy. This includes the basic practices of the Jedi. As well it will include lessons and ideas to help one live as a Jedi in their everyday life. Principles, practices, exercises one can easily follow. Now this is not going to be easy. I am not offering "be a Jedi Master in ten easy steps." It takes time, patience, discipline, and a lot of hard work. But it does work, it does help, and even if one is not a Jedi, they can take something useful from this book and their time reading it.

You may not find the Tao te Ching level of philosophical standards within this book. Yet you can find it within the Jedi

Path. We do not have any works which rival Marcus Aurelius's Meditations, the aforementioned Lao Tzu works, but this is not to say we can't or that the Path does not provide enough to eventually see these types of works spring from it. Jedi deal in ethics, they deal in world betterment, self-betterment, in how to approach life. They value and seek knowledge of all kinds and seek to understand the world around them through Jedi practices. We do not seek to answer the big questions as an path or organization. Creation of the Universe, Higher Power, Life After Death, these are left to the individual Jedi to sort through, to explore, to question themselves. The Jedi Path offers a solid foundation in which to explore these big concepts, but does not place one answer above another. In this Jedi is open religiously and why itself is not a religion (though people are free to take it as their personal religious view if they so choose).

HOW TO USE THIS BOOK:

Now something I'd like to mention is the change in the Jedi Circle's order. I will be listing the Jedi Circle in its current form in a bit. This order will be different than the order we are approaching it in the book. The format used we are starting with the Five Misconceptions as to address the major questions, problems, and concerns when dealing with the Jedi Path. This helps establish what the Jedi are not. Where our focus is and where it is not. This allows one a better understanding of what to expect and what we won't be getting into.

As this book is meant as a type of training guide this ordering is important. As such it is requested that you follow the order given. Of course as a book will it, not all will adhere to that. Some will jump to the sections that interest them the most. Or where they might be having an issue or question. Nothing to be done about that, the burden of book learning. Yet giving this order places an understanding of what a Jedi needs to focus on first.

The second part of this being a training tool is that there are pages with blank lines. Some do not like this addition. Yet I wanted to give space for those interested to keep tabs on their thoughts and practices. We will be offering assignments and exercises you can do if one so chooses. It simply seems logical to offer a place to record those elements without needing a new journal. Of course, you can get and start a Jedi journal, you can use the book, both, or neither. It is offered none-the-less.

Also in regards to the ordering we are listing the Tenets before the practices. In our online training program offered at the Jedi Academy Online we tackle practices much sooner. As they do play a vital part in the development and living of a Jedi. Yet again with book learning in mind it is simply better to approach core concepts such as Peace and Knowledge first as they offer a nice foundation of action. It is the simple idea that Power without Ethics, without Understanding is simply dangerous and foolhardy. So before we get into the meat and potatoes it is best to build that core foundation of why and how a Jedi acts.

I'll touch on a more on the creation of the Jedi Circle. We'll look at the Jedi Circle as it stands today. From there we will begin the exploration of each individual concept.

Jedi Circle History:

The Jedi Circle was created by myself, Opie Macleod (a.k.a Kevin Trout), in late 2004 during a turbulent time in my life. As such I couldn't get the right wording and feel that I wanted. As I returned to my basic studies of the Jedi Philosophy it started to become very clear to me. I wrote up the first draft and discussed it with my friend and roommate at the time Mindas Ar'ran. He felt it needed work, but showed a great start for breaking down and defining the Jedi Path.

In August 2005 the first version entitled Circle of the Jedi was released online at various Jedi Discussion websites. Places such as the Force Academy, JEDI, and Jedi Temple. The overall Jedi Community feedback was positive with a few suggestions and criticisms. Most felt the wording could be better, with some aspects seeming to repeat. For example awareness and observation were both used in the first draft. With the feedback from the Community (individuals who studied and live the Jedi Ideals daily) the Jedi Circle under went various changes. Over the years as the Jedi advance in their Path the Jedi Circle has evolved to reflect the changes.

At the time of this writing (2012) the Jedi Circle has been misused, misrepresented, chopped up, and stolen for over seven years. They say mimicry is the ultimate compliment, I imagine that goes for theft as well (have to want or admire something to go through the trouble of claiming it for your own). Overall it has been the best document for listing, explaining, and teaching the core foundation of the Jedi Path since its creation. It is not the end all, be all of the Jedi Path or our philosophy, but it is a great foundation for one to live their lives as Jedi in their everyday life.

The Jedi Circle is still at the heart of Jedi Academy Online Training Program. It is taught as the main standard for which all Jedi should compare themselves too. If you do not at least live by the Jedi Circle than you are simply not a Jedi. Again there is more to the training and living as a Jedi, but the Jedi Circle offers one a steady and respected guideline in which to follow the Jedi Ideals.

I have spent over 16 years in the Jedi Community, a total of 23 years self-study, and the Jedi Circle has lasted as a useful and accepted nonfiction Jedi Document for over seven years. It is this experience, this history that shows the worth and usefulness of the Jedi Circle in relation to the Jedi Path. I hope it offers some use and insight to you as well.

THE JEDI CIRCLE:

The Jedi walks the circle; S/he lives the Five Practices which enforce the Five Tenets, which nurture the Five Traits, which bring the Five Truths, which counteract the Five Misconceptions.

The Five Practices; *Meditation, Awareness, Diplomacy, Physical Fitness, and Self-Discipline.*

The Five Tenets; *Peace, Knowledge, Serenity, Harmony, the Force.*

The Five Traits; *Patience, Objectivity, Reliability, Humility, Wisdom.*

The Five Truths; *Self-Honesty, Learning, Guidance, Sacrifice, Commitment.*

The Five Misconceptions; *Star Wars, Religion, Compassion, Infallibility, Segregation.*

::The Five Practices::

Meditation: A Jedi practices meditation to quiet the mind, center the body, and connect the spirit. It is used to cultivate emotional well-being. Helping a Jedi cultivate calm, patience, and understanding.

Diplomacy: A Jedi seeks to resolve conflict before it

happens, to mediate misunderstandings, in this a Jedi practices diplomacy. Seeking to use intelligence, maturity, and words to end hostilities and pass on understanding.

Awareness: A Jedi practices awareness for the self and the world around them. We need to be aware of our own motives, limits, and desires. As well as those around us. Also if we are oblivious to the world around us, we may miss out on helping someone who truly needs it.

Physical Fitness: A Jedi practices physical-fitness for physical (and overall) well-being. Improved health, endurance to help out by physical means, and an in-depth understanding of the personal strengths and limits.

Self-Discipline: For a Jedi self-discipline is the cornerstone upon which the entire path is built. The ability to see things through, to complete our practices and honor our promises.

::The Five Tenets::

Peace: Peace is Acceptance. A Jedi must accept that there are things they have control over and things they do not. Peace comes from accepting our limitations, the limitations of others, and accepting to grow beyond them. Peace comes from accepting our emotions and not allowing them to rule our lives or decisions. Acceptance is Peace.

Knowledge: For a Jedi knowledge begins with the self, and works outward. We seek knowledge that we may better serve others. Though it may not relate to our Path, all knowledge is worth having. It is how we overcome the ignorance of our world.

Serenity: Serenity, finding inner calm and peace, especially when most needed. Serenity is about the mind remaining objective in the most extreme cases. Jedi cultivate serenity so that it may accompany them into the most hectic life.

Harmony: Moderation in all things. Excessive emotions, whether "positive" or "negative," create an imbalance within the self. We as Jedi seek Harmony in all things. Balance is key to a Jedi's life, balance between mind, body, and spirit. Balance between technology and nature. Harmony between ourselves, the Force, and the World we live in.

The Force: A suitable substitute for understanding is Life. The Jedi dedicate themselves to the Force, seeking to explore, experience and understand it. Through the Force we connect to the rest of the world and act accordingly as one connected entity.

::The Five Traits::

Patience: A Jedi must have patience. Not only in their training, but also in the world around them. With a little patience, many solutions will present themselves. "It is not necessary to always strike first, to provide the first solution, or to reach a goal before anyone else. In fact, it is sometimes vital to strike the last blow, to give the final answer, or to arrive after everyone else." - PotJ

Objectivity: A Jedi is a neutral party, looking at a situation from all sides. Regardless of one's position, a Jedi is unbiased. It is this objectivity that allows for clarity and understanding.

Reliability: A Jedi is one others may turn to in a time of need. They are there for others, whether emotionally, physically, or spiritually. They offer their guidance as best they can and provide a sturdy pillar to lean on when needed.

Humility: A Jedi is not above anyone else. A Jedi must remember that they are not better than the people they serve. We may train in self-betterment, and that may makes us different then some, but not above or better than anyone else.

Wisdom: While Jedi value and take care of knowledge, they understand that it takes wisdom to use knowledge properly. While Jedi may be seen as wise, they merely work from knowledge, experience, and the Force.

::The Five Truths::

Self-Honesty: Jedi know that control begins with the self. Through self-honesty they gain self-awareness, which gives self-knowledge, which helps in self-discipline. One cannot truly progress if they are not fully honest with themselves first.

Learning: Through continual learning, a willingness to always be a student, do we conquer ignorance. A Jedi recognizes that while they may master a certain field of study there is always more to learn in the world.

Guidance: Jedi spend years studying, reflecting, experiencing, both as individual people and as Jedi. In this they are able to offer guidance, whether acting as a signpost to the Jedi Way or giving advice to a friend. Jedi offer their guidance when requested.

Sacrifice: As Jedi we often have to make sacrifices at times. Giving of the self to help others. Using our personal time and resources to be there for others and continue our training. We give up certain freedoms to be Jedi. Such as the freedom to just lash out when angry, the freedom to deny someone help purely out of spite, and so forth.

Commitment: One can have self-discipline, but if they are not committed to the path they walk, then they will wander off it. In order to succeed at anything you have to be able and willing to see it through to the end.

::The Five Misconceptions::

Star Wars: Though the Jedi originate from the Star Wars mythos, it is not our sum. And one does not have to be a Star Wars geek or a Sci-Fi fanatic to become a Jedi. While Star Wars is our basis, it is not our reality. We, who live and walk the Path, define Jedi.

Religion: The Jedi Path is one open to all religious beliefs. Whether one follows Atheism, Christianity, Jediism, Taoism, or Zionism, regardless of belief if one follows and lives by the Jedi Path they are a Jedi. Overall the Jedi Path is a Way of life, a philosophy on how one lives. One does not have to follow or make Jedi their religion.

Segregation: People seek to create division, Jediism, Jedi

Realism, Jedi Pragmatism, Grey Jedi, Red Jedi, et cetera. However either one follows the Jedi Path and they are simply a Jedi. Or they do not follow the Path in which case they are not a Jedi. One Name, one Path, many roads. No need to separate or segregate, we all follow the Jedi Way.

Compassion: A Jedi must understand a situation and react properly to it. Adhering to the "There is no emotion; there is peace" ideals presented within the Jedi Code, we must be mindful of compassion. Like all emotions we feel it, but that does not mean it should influence our decisions. We should do the right thing, because it is the right thing, not because we an emotion compels us to. Or in shorter terms: Doing the Nice Thing and Doing the Right Thing are Not always the Same Thing.

Infallible: Jedi, no matter how powerful or clever, or how many years they have been training, are *not* infallible. There is nothing righteous or special about a Jedi, merely a person following and living a Path they deemed worthy. As Jedi we will fall and fail at times, but it is in picking ourselves up and continuing again that matters the most. Jedi understand Failure is not the end.

- Written by Opie Macleod (© 2004-2013 - Last update: December 12th 2011).

SECTION ONE: THE FIVE MISCONCEPTIONS -

::STAR WARS::

This will always be the biggest hurdle for the Jedi. Star Wars gave us the focus and inspiration. We were inspired to focus on something greater than ourselves. We seek to better ourselves so that we may in turn better the world around us. Which hopefully turns into bettering the entire world as a whole. Without Star Wars there would be no Jedi, no vision for a brighter future in this community, and all of us would be seeking our answers elsewhere, if at all. Honestly I have no idea where I'd be if it weren't for the ideal of becoming a Jedi Knight.

Yet it is also Star Wars that presents the biggest challenge. From the delusional who claim they can fly, to those that proclaim that Jedi must wear hoods on their heads when in public and activity pursue lawsuits in relation to that. From Religious Misunderstanding to Kids Playing Jedi online. Some of the biggest hurdles we face will be issues born of the fictional background of Star Wars.

Can you move things with your mind? How can Jedi exist in reality, weren't they simply soldiers for the republic government? Don't you have to wear robes? Where are the lightsabers? The questions are almost endless. Something that is important for all Jedi is being able to address fictional and ignorant concerns in relation to the Jedi and its inspiration Star Wars. This means understanding our common fiction, it means being able to draw the comparison and separate applicable information from the impossible. This is why we have the Jedi Lore section in tier three training.

Lets look at this from the Jedi Circle standpoint:
Star Wars: *Though the Jedi originate from the Star Wars mythos,*

it is not our sum. And one does not have to be a Star Wars geek or a Jedi fanatic to become a Jedi. While Star Wars is our basis, it is not our reality. We, who live and walk the Path define Jedi.

We will begin with covering the Misconception about the Jedi and their roots in Star Wars. Many of us have come to the Jedi path because of the Star Wars saga. And some of us have come despite of it. While the Jedi learn from the Star Wars mythos, we are not ruled by it. It is a framework from which to aspire. As such there is several differences between us and the Jedi you see in Star Wars.

First, any ideas of workable Lightsabers, Jedi Robes, or a Fancy Temple you can leave behind right now. Except for Halloween costumes and futuristic ideas, these have no place within our reality. We will not be fighting Dark Sith Lords or flying in Rogue Squadron. We will not be deflecting Force Lightning, or using the Force to move pears across the room. These cool special effects displayed in the movie may ignite the imagination, but they are not what a Jedi is.

Remember that even in Star Wars the Force did not define the Jedi. There were many Force-using paths in the fiction. What made the Jedi unique was their philosophy and way they lived. This is what separated them from other Force-Aspects.

Still, we share similarities with these Jedi as well. We dress within our times, we are exploring and studying the Force. We are keepers of peace and we will help those who request it. We train to better ourselves that we may live as Jedi and be of the most use when call upon. We learn from their fictional lessons and histories. From this we mold ourselves to be as Jedi Knights, no lightsabers, no Force Lightning, no cool robe, but the beginning of the Jedi none-the-less.

The Star Wars Mythology gives us valuable lessons, but do not adhere to it blindly. Many of what we teach and learn today is from the past 10 years of personal study of Jedi in today's society walking the Path of a Jedi. Some things from Star Wars serve us well, such as *"when calm, at peace."* This singular line

19

has been a basis for Jedi thought since it first made an appearance on the big screen. Is it applicable? Is it realistic? Certainly I feel each of us can think of a time when we made some poor choices out of anger and/or in haste. We knew the better option, but we were not calm, patient, at peace, we were driven by something that clouded our better judgment. Now obviously the philosophy is something much more boring then picking up a lightsaber and learning to fight. Learning to feel and enjoy being human and all the emotions that brings is a bit more important and just as taxing. At the same time being able to center ourselves, be at peace with ourselves, and make clear, calm, rational decisions even in the most heated situations is simply core to the Jedi lifestyle.

Other concepts have no place within our Path. Having a ruling body of 12 members because the Jedi Council was made of 12 members. Or "an apprentice you have Qui-Gon impossible to take a second." "The Code forbids it." Adopting that simply because it was a line in the movies? You have to look at relation, real-world application. For our organizations we need our administration to have an odd number for majority votes. Likewise our teacher to student ratio is off and to institute a rule of one apprentice at a time wouldn't be viable in many cases, especially at some of the other sites. Students seeking that Jedi mentor just would never get the chance due to the numbers.

Our terminology and inspiration may be from Star Wars but that is not all we are. We are the beginning, we are the scholars, priests, martial artist, monks, and philosophers that have come together under a single Path to build the foundations of the Jedi Way. At the same time, while we look to our inspiration for guidance, we have to make sure we are taking what is useful, practical, and applicable to our everyday lives.

::Section 1: L1 - Star Wars Homework Assignment::
Enjoy a little Star Wars time, watch the movies, play the games, read the books. Just take time to enjoy our common fiction. Than answer a few questions; What do you like the most about the fictional Jedi? What Jedi character do you most identify with

from the fiction? Are they your favorite character from Star Wars? If not who is? Name a quote you really like from whatever you watched, read, and/or played. How can these things be used to achieve real life goals, if at all? Explain your answers.

_____

_____

_____

_____

_____

_____

_____

_____

_____

_____

_____

_____

_____

_____

_____

_____

_____

_____

_____

_____

_____

_____

_____

_____

_____

_____

_____

_____

::RELIGION::

In the previous section we were exploring the difference between reality and fiction. In this section we are going to look at a misconception in the other direction; The Jedi Path as a Religion. In 2001 there was media attention to the Jedi Path. This was due to the U.K. Census and people listing Jedi as their Religion. A website Jediism Way, added to the fever of a Jedi Religion. People enlisted in the Military have listed Jedi as their religion to have it placed on their dog tags. In New Zealand a group of people has been known to hold "service" for those of the Jedi Religion. All this adds to the confusion of the question; Is Jedi a religion? Is there such a thing as Jediism?

One can say Jedi is *their* religion. One can follow the Jedi Way religiously. However this does not make it a religious institution. If one feels they follow the Jedi Path as their religion they may claim Jediism as their religion and that is perfectly acceptable.

Here at the Jedi Academy Online the view is that the Jedi Path is a lifestyle, it is a philosophy. It is a way we chose to conduct our lives within the world. There is no form of worship, no set doctrine, prayers or ceremonies. Could there be? Yes, it wouldn't be difficult to create a Jedi Religion, even a legitimate one. But the Jedi are not a religious organization, we are a philosophy, a belief in action. A diverse group of individuals who have come to train, learn, share and grow together. We share our different faiths and religions, even those that follow Jediism.

Out of the several Jedi in our community, our beliefs differ in terms of worship and religion. We have Jedi who are Christian, Wiccan, Catholic, Buddhist, Jewish, Muslim, Agnostic, and those who have a belief that doesn't fit into any organized religion. From this Jedi learn of different beliefs and cultures. While living as a Jedi you will come across many who have different beliefs and cultures, the first step in experiencing that is here with each other.

The Jedi Path is a Philosophical undertaking of living as a Jedi Knight. What we see in Star Wars is our biggest inspiration. And what we see are individuals who dedicated themselves to something that was within their ability to harness. It is this that separates us the most, the Jedi Path has no Deities, no prophets. Just good old fashion Human Ability.

In Star Wars the Force was not called or considered a God or a deity of any kind. Some would like to quote Han Solo "hokey religions and ancient weapons" and others quote Grand Moff Tarkin "You, my friend, are all that's left of their religion." These weren't meant to state Jedi was a religion, but to show the common misunderstanding of an outsider. They were not Jedi and had limited understanding of the Jedi. No Jedi has stated that the Jedi Path is a religion within the fiction. In fact there are Jedi who followed their own religion and cultural beliefs and customs. This was allowed within the fictional Jedi structure.

We are not looking to be a religion, we do not need to be one. We are not Scientology, we do not have worship or prayers or religious figureheads. Following a philosophical path is indeed a way of life, a core belief, but it is not a religion. We have our practices, we do not condemn others for their varied beliefs, we are simply not a religion. We are merely another path to walk in life.

This philosophy is something that speaks to certain people. It inspires them to grow and better themselves. They take it seriously, they train, study, practice, exercise, and overall grow as a person within the philosophy. It is a way of life they have chosen. A way of life which does not dictate their belief system. If an individual chooses to see the life energy of the world as God's creation than they are free to do that. If one wants to see the Force as the energy and impulses of the human brain and nervous system, they are free to do that.

No prayers are required here, just a desire to grow as a better person and the willingness to work hard for it. While some may find similarities between this philosophy and other religions, that is truly no surprise. Most religions have something in common with each other and they certainly all have something in common with the various philosophical schools of thought out there, altruism being an example.

Case and Point: We have no theories on the Creation of the Universe and/or Man. We have no Ritual Observance of Faith (no worship, no prayers, no holidays). We do not say what happens when you die (no after-life speculation); it could even be said we have no spiritual thought as energy can be seen as science, not spiritual idealism. After-all if we considered energy worth worship we would have to start praying to the Energizer Bunny. People may try to twist definitions to claim the Jedi Path as a religion, they may try to package it as some sort of universalism ideal of religion, may claim religious freedom to see it as a religion, but in the end it does not cover the basis that other religions do. At least that is what they have presented over the years in my experience.

What we must do now is see what your own studies uncover. Time to discover the answer for yourself. One last thing before we end here. As it is not know or clear. If one chooses to follow Jediism or say the Jedi is their religion, that is their choice. As mentioned, we do not tell any Jedi what to believe in terms of religion, from Atheism to Zionism - this includes one freedom to chose Jediism. However that is a personal choice and not on reflective of an entire Path or Organization.

::Section 1: L2 - Religion Homework Assignment::
Research the Jedi Religion, find examples of it, from youtube videos to various websites. Compare these with the basic foundations of the Jedi Path (Jedi Code, Jedi Circle, Jedi Rules of Behavior). Also research the word Religion - The word itself has various definitions and uses (context in which it can be used). Now come to your own conclusions as to whether or not the Jedi Path is a religion. Is the Jedi Path a Religion? Write your conclusions, in detail, in your journal.

::SEGREGATION::

From the Jedi Circle: *Some may view the Jedi Path as a Religion; however there is no set views on Creation, an Afterlife, or even a Deity. We have no holy dates, objects, people, or places. Being a Jedi is simply a lifestyle choice; choosing to live the Jedi Way. Not a religion.*

Originally this lesson was based upon the many Jedi "Aspects" that existed within our community. For years in our history it proved a problem. Shadow Jedi, Grey Jedi, Red Jedi, Dark Jedi, Forest Jedi, Water Jedi, Purple Jedi, Zen Jedi. These all existed as places and training groups at one time in our overall community. And the lesson here looked at each aspect and their varied ideals. What separated them, what they felt made them different, and their own development and studies.

The general idea behind the lesson was to show two things. One, that you either are a Jedi or you are not. Either you follow the Jedi ideals and Path and thus are indeed a Jedi, if you so wish to call yourself that. Or you did not follow the Path, but something similar, with similar inspiration, but ultimately did not walk the Path and thus were not a Jedi. The second thing was to show the evolution of understanding within the Jedi Path. How we progressed and how in that progress we saw less need to separate ourselves. As such segregation was more about claiming something individual, something elite, rather than anything that was actually different or needed.

However really only the Force Academy deals in Aspects of Jedi these days and even they tend to drop Jedi out of name. Instead of Shadow Jedi, they are a Shadow or Shadow Knight. The Dark Aspect you find Dark Knights, Sith, et cetera (though some minor groups of Shadow Jedi and Grey Jedi semi-exist out there still at this time of writing). Focusing on and teaching about the previous aspects is more a historical topic these days. Yet that doesn't mean we are not still segregated as a Path.

It seemed we had grown in understanding. As the Jedi

Community - Jedi was the key word and we finally as a group, as a community recognized that. That these glass walls of individuality were misguided - that it didn't matter what we believed as long as we followed the Path we have undertaken. But as one segregation fell away another rose in its place.

The Jedi have changed from aspects of color to aspects of faith. Now you will see that we separate ourselves by <u>Religion</u>, <u>Realism</u>, and what I personally call the <u>Pragmatists</u> (for lack of a better term). We will be exploring these main concepts of the Jedi. Learning a bit about what they believe, what they view the Jedi as, and how to get there. Also we will reference websites/organizations which tend to represent each aspect listed. This way we can research and get a better personal understanding of what each group believes.

We will start of with the Jedi religion, referred to as **Jediism**. Jediism itself is segregated a bit in actual belief and practices. Some say Jediism is a universal religion, a belief born of universal truths expressed within all religions. While others take a more direct view and believe the Force itself is a type of deity. Jediists, followers of Jediism, seek to have the Jedi recognized as an official religion. With the same rights and protections afforded to other religions such as Christianity, Judaism, Islam, and Buddhism. Some feel they have accomplished this with their individual organizations by gaining 501c(3) status with the United States IRS (Internal Revenue Service). This is a tax exempt for non-profit organizations 501c(3) specifically designed for Religious, Educational, Charitable, Scientific, Literary, Testing for Public Safety, to Foster National or International Amateur Sports Competition, or Prevention of Cruelty to Children or Animals Organizations.

As one can see, this does not mean one is a religion just because they have filed papers with the IRS. But it is the popular belief. Other groups, such as Church of Jediism in the United Kingdom has had a couple incidents where they cited religious discrimination. While never fully recognized as an actual religion they did receive an official apology from one of the incidents. The idea of being an actual religion is what defines Jediism against the other ideals we will be looking at.

Jediism is the newest kid on the block within the ideals. And that can often be seen within its training programs. They have been playing catch up (at the time of this writing), but still have not really met the standards of the Realist part of the Jedi. And that is due to the experience of the two groups. Jediism at first worked solely from the Master/Apprentice platform, but has since evolved into a Academy plus Apprenticeship format.

Generally you have titles and rank not only associated with the movies such as Jedi Masters, Grandmasters, and Knights. But also titles associated with Christian faiths such as Reverend, Bishop, and Brother.

Some groups that are most recognized as leaders of the Jediism movement are:

-= Temple of the Jedi Order =-
-= Church of Jediism =-
-= Jedi Church =-

Jedi Realism is a term that was adopted by Relan Volkum in lieu of the 2001 Jedi Census in the U.K. This is what caused mainstream attention to the Jedi and the term Jediism. In order to distinguish between the two lines of thought, Religion and Philosophical Ideal, Relan termed it Jedi Realism. The idea that we follow the philosophy as a guide in life, not a religion in itself. This also was done to promote the idea that Jedi are welcome from all walks of life. One can follow Christianity or any other religion as their form of faith and still be a Jedi. The two were separate things, the Jedi in fact could be seen as more of a supplement to one's own faith/belief.

The majority of sites which did not call themselves Jediism adopted this term. And now it is used as a clear distinction between the two ideals of Jedi Development. If one does not follow and/or agree with Jediism they tend to label themselves as a Jedi Realist. This used to be the majority of Jedi groups in the community. Even to the point of many using it for their name, such as the Jedi Realist Academy. The main distinction we see here is the acceptance that the Jedi is a philosophy, an ideal, an inspiration, not a religion.

Due to their long and varied history the Jedi Realist group forged ahead in terms of training and standards in the last few of years (2004-2008). However lately, the Jedi Realist groups have stagnated a bit in progress. Most use an Academy Format, and some still include an Apprenticeship thereafter, though the practice is dwindling. Though most Realists sites have not updated their training programs since 2008, if not older.

Most Jedi Realist groups use basic terms associated with the fiction such as Jedi Master, Jedi Knight, et cetera.
Some groups that are most recognized as leaders of the Jediism movement are:
-= The Force Academy =-
-= Institute for Jedi Realist Studies =-
-= Real Jedi Knights =-

Lastly we come to the most unknown and unfamiliar term, the **Jedi Pragmatists**.

This term came about in 2010 in a exploration of the major different views within the Jedi Community. At first there was only Jedi - no one cared whether it was a religion, or philosophy, we accepted differences and just went with a singular name. Then sides and colors were adopted to separate. And then Jediism came about and a line was drawn. Jediism and Realism these were the two defining points for years. But upon examination a new third class of Jedi was growing.

The Jedi Pragmatists grew out of the idea Jedi. Very similar to the Realists they hold to the idea that the Jedi Path is simply a Philosophical and Ideological way of life; not a religion. The difference is in execution, in focus, in training. Jedi Pragmatists don't really call themselves that, they simply call themselves Jedi. But for the sake of clarification another word was given to draw another clear line. Adding another glass wall to a community that seems it cannot do without them.

These Jedi have a higher standard then the other ideals presented. Because the focus is much more on real world application. Being a fully capable individual, not only being emotionally, physically, and mentally capable, but also social, and financially stable. As well as having the certification and legal rights to act within any situation.

This Jedi ideal grew out of the Realist Path to become something more useful, more practical. A focus on application and living as Jedi in our everyday lives.

Another clear difference is the use of titles. These Jedi tend not use the fictional titles of Jedi Knight or Master, but instead judge progress, experience, and knowledge, recognizing instead Levels of Jedi. One new to the Path starts at low level (such as Jedi of the First Level) and as they grow as a Jedi that is recognized via moving up to the next tier (such as Jedi of the Second Level).

The Jedi Academy Online, to the few who know of this place, is one of the defining sites of this classification of Jedi. However it is the stance of the Jedi Academy Online that all these terms are pointless. It does not matter what you believe as long as you follow the Jedi Path. If you live your life as a Jedi as best you can day in and day out, then you are a Jedi (period). Regardless what ism you want to place behind it, it is unnecessary, if you are a Jedi than you are a Jedi.

It is my personal stance that segregation is nothing more than our ego wanting to separate who is better. Who is more Jedi than the other, who is more enlightened, who is more capable, without actually having to say that. Jedi - do we need more than that? This was confirmed in 2011 with a community-wide project in which I traveled to the various websites around the community and sought their opinion on dropping all "isms". Jediists said they would not because it distinguishes them from the Realists and they want that because they are better. Seriously, their words. I would write what Realists said, but it is just as easy to say, they said the exact same thing.

Now the question becomes - is that true? Is there an actual difference? Sure, there are some. Titles, training standards, programs, they differ. But the core ideals, the core beliefs and practices? No. Jediism tends to have more spiritual focus. Realism tends to have more supernatural focus. But Peace, Knowledge, Serenity, Harmony, the Force. Meditation, Physical Fitness, Diplomacy, all these are core to all "*isms*." Time for your own explorations and conclusions.

::Section 1: L3 - Segregation Homework Assignment::
You have spent some time in the Jedi Community, take awhile to merely observe its workings, its flow. Take a look at the various different sites in the Jedi Community, we have given some to start at. Question from that: Are the Jedi Segregated? Or are they merely diversified? Both? Is Diversity and Segregation the same thing? Is Diversity a strength within the Jedi? Is Segregation a Strength (if they do not mean the same thing in your opinion)? Why? Explain your answers.

::COMPASSION::

"A Jedi must understand a situation and react properly to it. Adhering to the "There is no emotion; there is peace" ideals presented within the Jedi Code, we must be mindful of compassion. Like all emotions we feel it, but that does not mean it should influence our decisions. We should do the right thing, because it is the right thing, not because an emotion compels us to."

First, know that a Jedi can feel and have compassion. This is important, because a Jedi is not an uncaring robot. A Jedi must see the difference between doing something because it is the proper action to take and doing something because they feel sympathy for one's plight. We must be able to look at a situation objectively and determine the best course of action for all involved. Sometimes our helping isn't the nice guy option, the nice thing to do. At other times, it really is.

Jedi do not take pity on people, that is not what we do and it is not the reason we should seek to help others. Two points to remember here, one a Jedi helps others to help themselves. Two, a Jedi acts from reason not emotion. A Jedi looks at an entire situation taking in all angles and all individuals involved. They understand that as humans we have emotional investments. Talking with your best friend about his unsteady relationship, you feel for him. Yet as a Jedi you have to be open to all possibilities and not allow your friendship and compassion to cloud your judgment or your advice.

Compassion has compelled people to do some really heroic actions in our world. It has also compelled people to be used and swindled. Yet a Jedi does not need that push forward. A Jedi sees a situation and understands what should be done, and then does it. Understanding a situation for what it is has more value than acting from a desire to end one's suffering. You have to remain objective and open to the situation at hand.

Why does a Jedi help? Simple, because they can. If we

have the ability to do something then we have the responsibility to do something. Not out of compassion or pity, but because it is the proper thing to do. We are there and can do something, so we will. It is as simple as that, act from understanding. Observe, Understand, Act Accordingly. Apply the Jedi Method here.

Compassion, it is a tricky topic to cover. Many people like the idea of compassionate individuals. Some of the greatest people in our history are compassionate and speak highly of the trait. Yet I feel that most overlook the problem with compassion, it is an emotion that can easily blind one to the objective nature of any situation. We should seek understanding of situations, rather than having sympathy for it.

We feel for people at times, we understand the pain they are going through. Yet it is that understanding that will serve best. By remaining objective we can offer more clear advice and direction without taking away from their own experience and ability to stand on their own two feet. It is understanding the entire situation, seeking information that will give us the best idea of how to proceed.

The idea of the Jedi is empathy not sympathy. You can perform compassionate acts without being emotionally compelled or compromised. Jedi embrace their emotions. We seek emotional stability and well-being. We do not deny how we feel or what we feel. Yet at the same time we do not act solely off that emotion. When mad we do not act based off that anger. We take a second. Acknowledge our feelings, process them, and then act. It is no different with compassion.

Compassion tugs at our heart strings begging for action now, without thought or consideration to the entire situation. Compassion leads us to give a man a fish, rather than to teach him how to fish. We seek the most immediate solution rather than work for a permanent course of action.

When presented with a situation that screams from compassionate hearts and minds, take a step back and look at it objectively, seek the solution from a fair and calm standpoint. Seek to understand the problem from all sides and then look to fix it.

<u>Zen Story:</u>
Several monks at a monastery had noticed a deer grazing nearby and so they began to feed it scraps of food. After a while the deer became trusting and would even eat out of the hands of the monks. Thus the monks were pleased with themselves however when their abbot found out he was less then happy and so when a suitable opportunity arose he threw sticks and stones at the deer which ran away frightened as the abbot wanted.

::Section 1: L4 - Compassion Homework Assignment::

Question 1: In the story above. Is compassion shown to the deer in this story? Why? How did you come to this conclusion?
Question 2: If there is a compassionate party, which one is it and why?
Scenario 1: You are walking down the street. Homeless Man asks for change. What do you do and why?
Scenario 2: Knock at your door. You answer it. It is a teenage boy. Dressed averagely for one of his age. He informs you that he performing a school project for the arts. If he raises enough money he will be able to go to the Chicago Art Institute for a visit and learn about their program, with a potential scholarship. All he needs is some magazines subscriptions. He goes on to thank you for not being rude, slamming the door in his face, and so on. He is well-mannered and polite. After chatting for a little bit he expresses his worry about raising enough to fulfill his dream. What do you do? And why?
Scenario 3: You are driving to work (or school). In a bit of hurry, but no more than usual. The street is three lanes, you are in the middle lane. Traffic is more backed-up than usual however. It seems slow for no apparent reason. You get to the light that seems to be holding people up and you notice in the slow lane (or number 1 lane) a car is stalled with its hazard lights on. What do you do? And Why?

::INFALLIBILITY::

"Jedi must understand that failure should never be the end. The Jedi Path places a heavy load on the Jedi, requiring almost superhuman traits for them to accomplish all it demands. In large and small ways, all Jedi eventually fail the challenges posed by the Path. They might act in anger or succumb to temptation. They might work against the balance of the Force, even with the best intentions. They will fall from the high ideals they hold.

True failure of a Jedi is not in stumbling or failing to live up to the ideals of the Order. The true failure occurs if, once having fallen, the Jedi fails to rise again. Jedi strive to live up to the Jedi Code and the teachings of their Masters. When (not if, but when) a Jedi fails to attain those goals, the only choices are to let the failure dominate her life, or to rise from the ashes of that defeat and strive to make peace with himself through the Force. That is the Way of the Jedi." Power of the Jedi Sourcebook Almost want to leave that as the entire lesson.

Fear, Disgust, Ignorance, Disappointment, Anger, Shock, and the out-right "I want to destroy the world."

The point is that these are things you have felt and will feel again. A Jedi, no matter how literal they follow the Jedi Code, is not perfect and will fail as a Jedi. We understand it is not feeling an emotion, but it is how we act on it that matters. It is one thing to feel angry and another to react in anger. As Jedi we must acknowledge our state-of-mind and act accordingly. And there will be a time when you fail.

Look we ask a lot of <u>You</u> as a Jedi. We say - Awareness, it means multiple things, from situational awareness, emotional awareness, to awareness of the self. We expect you to follow all of them. Peace and knowledge have multiple meanings and you must know and follow all of them. You must overcome over-confidence, arrogance, aggression. You must follow the Jedi

Code, Jedi Circle, Jedi Method, and Jedi Rules of Behavior. That is a lot of information. A lot to live by and a lot to live up too. Fact: You will fail in this endeavor more then once.

Is that an excuse to fail? To continue to fail? No. It is not okay per se, it is simply a statement of fact. Yet as a Jedi you must seek to learn from the mistake and not allow it to repeat again. Mistakes, Errors, 20/20 Hindsight, they do happen. What you must do is not regret, but accept. Learn from it so that it does not become a regular or normal course of action. You may react out of anger without thought - definitely a Jedi no-no. Learn from it, examine it, why did you lose control, why were you unable to retain your calm, truly look at it honestly, objectively, learn and grow.

For 23 years I have studied the Jedi Path. For over 16 years I trained, taught, learned, and lived as a Jedi. I cannot count the mistakes I have made, they are simply too numerous. That is the the purpose of this academy, of training in this style. Learn from my mistakes, my failures, my inabilities, and become better than myself. Surpass the Teacher. The best way to do that is to learn from our mistakes without repeating them yourself. Jedi are not perfect, but we can certainly set a higher standard for ourselves.

We can set a high bar. We can accept we will always be striving for that bar and may never reach it. But that does not make it any less worth trying for. No Jedi is perfect, no Jedi is infallible, we are simply individuals who continually better ourselves and strive for that self-betterment.
From the Jedi Circle:

Infallible: *Jedi no matter how powerful or clever, or how many years they have been training, are NOT infallible. There is nothing righteous or special about a Jedi, merely a person following and living their beliefs. And Jedi will fall and fail at times, but it is in picking themselves up and continuing again that matters the most. Jedi understand Failure is not the end.*

You are going to snap, in a small way such as screaming at your parents. Or in a big way, unleashing your anger on someone

40

and beating them into the ground.. Is this condoned? No. And punishments should be given accordingly. But if we judged everyone off of the mistakes they make in life, none of us would be here. It is learning from these mistakes, taking the lesson and experience and applying it to our lives. Facing our demons and doing right by them.

We face hardships and trials everyday on many levels. It is learning from these trials, growing from these hardships that shape us. *"Your focus determines your reality."* Do not be kept down because you may slip or fail, be stronger for it. You will always have the Jedi Community to turn to, your fellow peers, and friends.

Look whenever we change how we do things, from how we live to how we cook chicken Parmesan we need to expect some problems. Change your route to work? Expect some extra time getting there your first day. We are taking a risk, we are altering what is normal and comfortable to us. There are going to be some bumps. This however is not necessarily bad. Trial and error tend to offer more learning, progress, and growth. What will always be important is **how** you deal with your failure.

::Section 1: L5 - Infallibility Homework Assignment::
Reflection time. Consider your time living and training as a Jedi, what mistakes have you made? Did you learn from them or are you repeating them? Now, even further, consider your life and think of all the mistakes. Reflect on them, take what lessons you can from them, are these the same lessons you took form them when they happened? All this is just to help you understand the value in our mistakes and the desire to not repeat them
Exercise
Pick three failures. Write them out 1-2-3. Then write the lesson learned from them 1-2-3. And at the end answer, were these failures valuable learning experiences for you?

_____

_____

SECTION TWO: THE FIVE TENETS -

::PEACE::

Peace is Acceptance. A Jedi must accept that there are things they have control over and things they do not. Peace comes from accepting our limitations, the limitations of others, and accepting our ability to grow beyond them. Peace comes from accepting our emotions and not allowing them to rule our lives or decisions. Acceptance is Peace.

What we are talking about here is not the ever elusive Peace you hear about in Meditation seminars or some new age book. It is peace of mind that we are talking about and that we are all looking for. Peace of mind is all that we truly need to get by in this chaotic world, but it can be hard to obtain. Many seek peace at some retreat or seminar, but these things can only help you escape. They do not teach you how to attain peace where it counts, in the middle of your hectic life. Peace is easy enough to accomplish when removed from the noise of this world, but what good is that unless you live in the mountains away from everything?

No, peace of mind does not serve anyone unless you can have it in the middle of chaos. What we want is to be in the whirlwind of society dealing with meetings, bills, family, and general everyday stress and still be calm and at peace within ourselves. You cannot maintain the objectivity needed when you are constantly dealing with inner-conflict. So now that we have addressed what exactly we are talking about here and where we need it most, the question becomes, how do we reach this peace of mind?

Before we directly answer that. Lets look at what we are talking about for Jedi. Peace for a Jedi has a two-fold meaning.

The first is as many people view it; Peace not War. Peaceful surroundings, peaceful solutions, world peace. And while we do not have the power to make all these things a reality, it is something Jedi value and strive for. Using diplomacy and mediation as a means of conflict resolution instead of using force. Jedi value peace and seek to present ways to express this ideal, both on an individual level and a more global level.

Yet this is not the only meaning of the word Peace. The Jedi seek to cultivate the other side of peace; inner peace. Peace of mind, not so much within themselves, but at the root of any conflict they come across. In order to attain and maintain this peace, Jedi work to have a clear and peaceful demeanor in order to express the value of peace without being clouded by emotions or bias.

Peace within in order to affect peace in our surroundings; inner peace to affect the outer world. *"Peace born of anger is no peace at all, and cannot last."* - Power of the Jedi Sourcebook. This peace goes much deeper than external conflicts. It is peace found within. We all have huge inner conflicts and thoughts, we often struggle with ourselves more than any one else. Thus a Jedi seeks to find internal peace just as much as they seek external peace. Thus you have the two-fold of peace; External conflict resolution and Internal conflict resolution, both seeking to attain a peaceful outcome.

But knowing about peace and achieving peace are two different things. So how does one reach this so-called peace? Practice, patience, tolerance, understanding, listening, diplomacy, self-honesty, and the ability to look at all sides, even when our own ego is involved. In the end though remember, Peace is Acceptance. We must **accept** that there are things we have control over and things we do not. Peace comes from accepting our limitations, the limitations of others, and growing beyond them. Accepting our beliefs and role, and accepting the beliefs and roles of others. Accepting the world we live in and our own role in that world. **Peace comes from accepting our emotions** and not bottling them up or allowing them to rule our lives or decisions.

Peace is Acceptance. It is what we strive for daily. Peace within themselves, peaceful resolutions, a state of peace (without conflict).

Things anger us, people upset us, injustices can make us cry. We get mad at people and events, often things way outside our realm to control or effect in any way. We struggle, rebel, we rage against the world we live in, against the decisions other people make. We can seek to force people into doing what we "*know*" to be good for them. Becoming a tyrant and enforcing our ideals on others because we cannot accept their decisions. It all comes down to acceptance. That starts with the self and grows outwardly. Once we can and have accepted the whole (the self and the entire world as is) then we can make clear objective decisions on how best to proceed.

You have to understand yourself. Your motivations. You must be willing to accept yourself. Our emotions aren't to be banished. They are not enemies of peace. They are a core part of us. They serve a valuable purpose within us. This doesn't mean one should act rashly on their emotions. Simply that our emotions do not threaten our peace. Be at peace with your emotions. Acknowledge them, accept them, embrace them. It is okay to feel. It is okay to be mad or sad or happy or tired. It is okay and you can still have that peaceful center within yourself without sacrificing your emotions or how you feel.

Again, lets cover this thoroughly. "*I cannot believe she would call me fat!!*"One should strive to accept the world and people for who and what they are. Some people are just selfish and petty, that is their right. The world sometimes lashes back claiming hundreds of lives. And each time we want to point the finger to someone or something and blame them. But blame can be passed anywhere. A better way is simply to accept. That is remembering we are each entitled to our life, our faults, mistakes, and beliefs.

Through acceptance we can accept our place within this crazy world and with the people who live in it. Things happen everyday, good things, bad things, events are unfolding right now.

Many have died since you started reading this. Many in not so pleasant ways. And yet, many are born, many are celebrating, the world is full of events in every second. The key is to accept all things, including yourself. And here is is a hint as to how:

Do not allow the things you can change to upset you. Why? Because you can change them, you can do something and make a difference. All you have to do is exercise some of that self-discipline. Things may not work out how you want or the way you wanted, but accept you will do and did your best. Now, on the same note, do not allow the things you cannot change to upset you. Why? Because you cannot change them. There are several events in human history, most tied to war, which spark outrage and sorrow. Understand now, you cannot change those events. They are done and you need to accept that, be at peace with it. The world, human and nature alike, strikes hard and without mercy at times. Once we accept it, acknowledge our feelings on said events, we can then move forward and react in a proper and beneficial manner.

Even if you are standing right there when something happens, the event is done. It was not prevented. So your only focus at that time is what you need to do at that time. A child gets hit by a car in front of you. Accept the event and move forward. Do not seek to get upset or angry. Do not look to pass blame on someone. Instead merely focus on the facts, what needs to be now. Medical help, making sure all relevant facts are remembered. How it happened, what was going on before, during, after. People that saw, people involved, get the information as best you can well helping those you can. Pictures, authorities, help, do what you can. Acknowledge, Accept, Move Forward. By accepting and moving on you can remain calm and objective. In this you will be at peace and work towards peace.

::Section 2: L1 - Peace Homework Assignment::

When you feel emotions coming up, whether in reflection or within the moment I want to you acknowledge those feelings. Understand that they are natural and thank yourself for bring these signs to your attention. Accept how you feel, do not bottle up your emotions, and move forward. Move to the next step - what now?

Be sure to take a moment if you need it. Count to 10, breathe deeply. Remember, what would a Jedi do? Objectivity, Calm. Really seek to cultivate this over the next week.

_____
_____
_____
_____
_____
_____
_____
_____
_____
_____
_____
_____
_____
_____
_____
_____
_____
_____
_____
_____
_____
_____
_____
_____
_____
_____
_____
_____

::KNOWLEDGE::

Knowledge has a couple different layers which relate to the Jedi. First and foremost self-knowledge, *"know thy self."* A Jedi must know their own limitations, strengths, weaknesses, fears, doubts, talents, and overall abilities. It is not something gained after a single night of reflection; however seriously sitting down and really, truly, examining yourself will produce some great results in one night. For a Jedi though it is one night repeated for the rest of your life.

Yet knowledge of self is only one part of being a Jedi. Knowledge in general is a very important factor to all Jedi. *"All knowledge becomes useful."* - Sherlock Holmes. For a Jedi this statement is truth. Yet one should consider the words of Albert Einstein when he said *"A little knowledge is dangerous. So is a lot."* The responsibility of knowledge lays on the shoulders of those that seek it. For a Jedi they understand that Knowledge may be dangerous, but ignorance can and has killed.

C.P.R., Heimlich maneuver, A.E.D., these are things that various professionals are taught (medical, emergency response teams, Police officers, and even security officers). Yet they are also a leading cause of death, because most people do them incorrectly. Ignorance, misunderstanding, and lack of self-knowledge have and do lead to more problems within situations.

A Jedi seeks to gain knowledge, applying knowledge where applicable, sharing knowledge when it would serve best, and reserving knowledge when necessary. Through the respect of knowledge and the continual search for knowledge Jedi develop a deep understanding of various subjects and trades, as well as a deep understanding of themselves as individuals.

Attaining knowledge is not difficult at all. First before learning about anything, remove anything you think you know about it. Always start fresh with a beginner's mind, approach things with a open viewpoint allowing people to show and instruct you on their way of doing things. After you are able to approach each new thing as a brand new thing, than ask questions, seek clarification. From here you will be gathering knowledge over and over. Save it, write it down, record it, this allows knowledge to be reviewed and passed on to others. Knowledge is simply picking something and learning it, history, philosophy, how to bake cookies. Truly the list is endless, especially taking into account that different people often do the same task differently. Take some time and learn something new.

::Section 2: L2 - Knowledge Homework Assignment::

Knowledge, we all have it in one form or another. And yet we are also all ignorant in certain subjects as well. So our assignment is two-fold:

1.) Pick a subject you feel rather versed in. Perhaps it is a hobby, like sewing. Maybe it is a game like Pokemon. Maybe it is a passion such as local wildlife. A subject in school you excel in - history, math. Reflect on the things you consider yourself knowledgeable in. Pick one and share some of that knowledge - educate me, a laymen (in whatever you chose), on the subject. A introductory lesson.

2.) I want you to pick either a big historical event or a religion that you know basically nothing about. Even one you wanted to learn more about, because you knew only a little. I want you to research it. Study the event or beliefs. What did you choose? Why did you choose it? What did you learn? In learning about it were any misconceptions changed? Et cetera, feel free to be as in-depth as you like.

3.) How is knowledge (in general) useful to a Jedi?

_____

_____

_____

_____

_____

_____

::SERENITY::

Serenity is often seen as the exact same as peace and thus redundant in the Jedi Philosophy. Yet this is hardly the case. While peace does have a similar aspect in the idea of peace of mind or inner peace, serenity does not relate to the cession of war. No, when we speak of serenity we are speaking of something within our being. <u>Where Peace is Acceptance, Serenity is Stillness.</u>

"Deep in the soul, below pain, below all the distraction of life, is a silence vast and grand- an infinite ocean of calm which nothing can disturb; Nature's own exceeding peace, which 'passes understanding.' That which we seek with passionate longing, here and there, upward and outward; we find at last within ourselves."
- R M Bucke

While I would use this quote to explain peace to a Jedi as well, it more accurately describes how the Jedi should be on the inside. Serenity, a vast ocean of calm within ourselves even in the most chaotic of situations we find our entire being and mind calm and still. An undisturbed lake at 5am, peaceful, serene.

Serenity for a Jedi is the calm objective center of being we seek at all times. It is our balance to emotions and passions of life. While a Jedi feels the normal wide variety of emotions and has plenty of topics on which they are passionate about, they seek and create a balance within themselves which is counteracted with serenity.

Serenity compared to Peace, which is often debated, is merely that peace used much more in relation to inner and outer battles. Peace within the self is sought to end inner conflict. In this we are better able to handle all outer conflicts which arise. And serenity is the tool we use to foster inner peace, to maintain that delicate balance within ourselves. To stay human and enjoy life, but to be calm and objective enough to handle all situations with a clear and serene mind and spirit.

Serenity is often said to best be achieved by meditation. And while that will certainly help,the best thing for serenity is to get some YOU time. It is important to have an outlet or you will go crazy no matter what you do. Movies, Video Games, Hiking, Swimming, Water Skiing, anything, something, all of these. Do not neglect the down time your body, mind, and spirit need. You work-out, you allow you body to rest. You stress yourself out, you need to allow your mind to do the same. And encourage those around yo to do the same.

Meditation is great to de-stress, but so is a hot shower with loud music, a bubble bath, a cartoon, a video game, a good book, a midnight stroll in your own backyard. What is important is what works for you and you take the time to enjoy it. You cannot force yourself to relax, just allow it the chance to happen. When you achieve that than you will be able to cultivate serenity within yourself. Knowing you have that refillable ocean of calm within you. Just remember to fill up again.

::Section 2: L3 - Serenity Homework Assignment::

Serenity - Seek to obtain it. Take some "you" time and just enjoy your time for awhile. Do something you find relaxing and enjoyable. Master the Art of Doing Nothing. Take the next week and cultivate your Serenity. Build that inner spring-well of calm that you may draw upon it when things get hectic.
Simply write your reflections, thoughts, and insights on serenity and personal calm.

_____

_____

_____

_____

_____

_____

_____

_____

::HARMONY::

Harmony, balance, equilibrium. Jedi seek harmony throughout their training and this balance comes in a variety of forms. Balance between, home, work, and training, balance between experiencing emotions and being controlled by them. It is a continual state of change in which one must maintain balance. Jedi seek harmony between technology and the Eco-system. A Jedi will have to balance understanding with tough love at times. We cannot always be the shoulder to cry on, at times we have to help that person stand on their own two feet. That is not always an easy task, it is not always understood, and it requires the Jedi to balance several emotional and diplomatic factors in a singular situation.

We hear the saying, *"all things in moderation."* And this is something that we all hold to be true. Physical activity is good to keep us fit and active, too much can destroy our bodies, making them age beyond their time. A drink with a friend at a bar can be fun, yet allowing alcohol to come before marriage and loved ones is a problem. All things in moderation and that means setting up a balance in life with everything you do. Being dedicated to your work is great and will most likely pay off, but make the time for yourself and those you care about.

We get so busy and stressed out with everything in life we forget to maintain that ever important harmony within life. Moderation in the things we enjoy, the things we need to do, and the things we chose to do (such as a healthy diet to better ourselves). Too much of any one thing will tear you down, even the Jedi Path. As Jedi we live the Jedi Path 24 hours a day, 7 days a week, and that can get to the best of us. Does this mean you have breaks from the Jedi? No, what it means is that you create a balance, allow yourself to put down the training (books, sparring gloves, Internet, etc) and just enjoy a bit of life. Laugh at a good joke, remember why we train, to protect those around us and safeguard the things we love about life.

Okay so we all know how chaotic and crazy life can get. The world continues to turn and bury with stuff no matter how much we are already suffocating. This is no surprise, it is life. And it may overwhelm people, it may get the better of people, but the question is, what will do you about it?

Sure, I suppose venting helps, going to your friends having a rant, and than re-focusing yourself thereafter. Yet as Jedi we are guided by certain principles, certain ethics. One of the major tenets of that philosophy is There is no Chaos; there is harmony.

As Jedi we seek balance with life and the world around us; no matter how much you may dislike it. Being a Jedi is not about loving the world, or being an optimist, it is about living as a Jedi regardless of the state of the world. And that means facing a world that would crush you at the next turn and still helping others.

As said life is chaos, Jedi find the balance within themselves and the world around them. They find balance with technology and nature, they find balance between brutal truth and rose tinted glasses. We know the world is not perfect, neither are we, thus we live life for many years gaining that experience, wisdom, and insight. And with any luck be able to pass it on to those willing to listen.

So when it seems too much, fall back to the basics. Be a Jedi, seek harmony.

How does one attain such harmony within their life? Continual practice, and that is about it. Pace yourself, watch yourself, come you learn when enough is enough. And know that the world is not ending tomorrow. Have fun, but remember that fun will be waiting for you to return, so handle your business in the meantime. Be the Jedi, train as a Jedi, but remember that Jedi are alive and thus have lives too. Enjoy that life, do something with it, just remember and always practice: Moderation in all things.

::Section 2: L4 - Harmony Homework Assignment::

Spend a week observing your habits, keeping in mind the saying 'all things in moderation.' During that time seek to find a balance within yourself and your surroundings. Balance diet, balance physical, mental, and spiritual well-being, balance technology with nature (recycling, walking to the store, etc). After that reflect and put into practice the ideals of balance and harmony.
Answer: What is Harmony? How do you strive and obtain Harmony? What part does harmony play in the Jedi Path?

_____

_____

_____

_____

_____

_____

_____

_____

_____

_____

_____

_____

_____

_____

_____

_____

_____

_____

_____

::THE FORCE::

The Force is many things to many people. In fact some take a view that it is indeed a singular thing which has been divided and call many names; such as Ki, Chi, Mana, Prana, the Holy Spirit, Fighting Spirit, Life Force, et cetera. We come to a point where many in our Path simply stick to the classic Star Wars quotes, such as *"The Force is what gives a Jedi his power. It's an energy field created by all living things. It surrounds us and penetrates us. It binds the galaxy together."* And the classic, *"For my ally is the Force, and a powerful ally it is. Life creates it, makes it grow. Its energy surrounds us and binds us. Luminous beings are we, not this crude matter. You must feel the Force around you; here, between you, me, the tree, the rock, everywhere, yes."*

My personal experience tends to support those fictional quotes. But the Force can be looked at from many viewpoints. We can and have approached it scientifically, looking at what verifiable facts we can about the many kinds of energy. Energy comes in a couple different forms, kinetic, thermal, not to mention how our body processes food and turns that into energy for our body. We can look at the Force as simply the beauty of the Brain and workings of life. Simply a process of enhancing our own latent abilities and refining our used abilities such as our five senses. It can be found in the physics which we know to be true.

This is why we often refer to the Force as the Ineffable. Our goal as Jedi is to get a better understanding the Force. To come to actual conclusions in the future. That takes a formula of Exploration, Experience, and Definition. When we are able to reach tangible, repeatable results via this method we will start to point a finger on the grand idea of the ineffable. But it is truly unlikely we will ever have a clear and full understanding of the Force. And will always leave some of the Force to personal definition and belief.

Looking at the classic Star Wars view of the Force is not a bad place to start our journey. It is vague, open, and allows for a very broad view of what we call the Force. And this is our starting point: "*Life creates it, makes it grow. Its energy surrounds us and binds us.*" Life creates energy in many forms, even in the purely scientific sense. With view we also get a main and important statement: <u>We Are All Connected.</u> This should be considered when interacting with others, when reacting to events, from how you address people to how you handle situations; remember that we are all connected in life.

It is this aspect of being connected that seems the most important for Jedi Philosophy. Regardless how one may view the Force, what all Jedi can agree on is the beauty of connected action. What one person does affects the entire whole. With this in mind we get a better sense of proper action versus improper action. If a person meets a Jedi for the first time and that Jedi loses it, does something harmful. What does that person now think of all Jedi? How many Jedi would it take to correct that one bad experience? The actions of one have affected the whole.

If one approaches the Force as nothing else but a metaphor they still again valuable insight into living and acting as a Jedi. This is key to remember in our diverse community. The Force is a guiding force for the Jedi regardless of how a Jedi explains it, uses it, or the practices they associate with it; as long as those fall within the Jedi Philosophy, the Force is yours to define.

::Section 2: L5 - The Force Homework Assignment::
Take a week to meditate on the quotes given in this lecture and observe life as well. Seek to sense and understand the flow of life around you. Take times through out the week to simply close your eyes and seek to feel the Force, life, around you. Look for the connections in life, big and small. At the end of the week write in your own words about your experiences and how you describe what the Force is, based upon your experiences.

SECTION THREE: THE FIVE PRACTICES -

:: SELF-DISCIPLINE::

Self-discipline, without it a Jedi would never be a Jedi, it is truly as simple as that. A Jedi practices and maintains their self-discipline daily, after-all we do not always like to wake-up and work-out every morning. Meditate when we need too, sometimes we just want to get mad, and be lazy. Yet the Jedi lifestyle warns against such things, even small allowances can be dangerous. So, as Jedi, we do it any way. We train, we practice, we study, and we do our best in life.

In life we will come across situations where we do not want to get involved. Where we feel it is not our place or we just really have somewhere else we want to be. We notice traffic is backed-up on the street more than usual, when we get closer we notice the cause is a person's car has broken down in one of the lanes. You are on your way home from a very stressful day. This is the last thing you want to deal with. And if you stop to help, your car may get damaged by a careless driver.

It is the responsibility and self-discipline of the Jedi that will dictate the outcome of this little scenario. You are a Jedi, this is more than within your ability to help and fix. And so, you just do it, as the Nike commercials used to say. You do what needs to be done, you take the time to get out and push the car to safety. It is not a hard choice, but often times one we just do not wish to make. Yet that is what will separate us every time.

Self-discipline is another one of those hard subjects for a Jedi to be taught. I cannot tell you how to develop self-discipline outside of just doing it. There are some things I can give which encourage the practice. And can help you organize yourself into making sure you get done what you need/want to get done. Here are some helpful tips:

- Put your plans on paper. Spell out your goals and ways to reach them.
- Be specific. The advice you give yourself must be such that you can put it into practice.
- Break the task down into small pieces so that you can handle them easily.
- Establish checkpoints on your progress as well as rewards. Remind yourself of the benefits you expect from your tasks completion.
- Avoid temptations and circumstances that might sidetrack you.
- Recognize your limitations. Don't set unrealistic goals. Take advantage of your own energy peaks!
- Use negative motivation. Remind yourself of the consequences of inaction.
- Keep a time-control budget. Don't let one task take control over others.
- Set deadlines and hold yourself to them.
- Make an honest distinction between "I can't" 📄 and "I don't want to".
  Get started now. Don't stall.
- Improve your self-persuasion ability. Learn the difference between reasoning and rationalizing.
- Be optimistic. Your chances for success will increase.
- Decide how you want to start, what needs to be done first. Read, especially literature related to your situation.
- Use self-signaling devices - notes, signs, cues, reminders.
- Use the stimulation provided by good news to do extra work.
- Recognize conflicts and make a choice.
- Give yourself the right to make mistakes. No one is perfect.
- Exercise your sense of humor. Laughter indicates a

realistic point of view.

In the end it is merely up to yourself. You just have to hold yourself to it, make yourself go through with it. Work-out even when you do not want too. Meditate even though you would rather watch a movie. The list is truly endless, just do it.

::Section 3: L1 - Self-Discipline Homework Assignment::

For the next Week you are to pick one thing you dislike doing or have chosen not to do and do it. Example: Dishes. If you never or rarely wash the dishes, you are on Dish Duty for the next 7 days. Mowing the Lawn? Shoveling the snow? Pick a chore you seek to avoid and for one complete week do that chore continually and as best as possible. What chore/charity did you chose? Did you follow through all seven days? What did you do with your time, if not? Any thoughts or reflections?

_____

_____

_____

_____

_____

_____

_____

_____

_____

_____

_____

_____

_____

_____

_____

_____

_____

_____

::DIPLOMACY::

Diplomacy is the first tool and defense of the Jedi. Information, knowledge, and a quick wit allow us to use words as a weapon. We must listen before we can speak. And if there is one major rule to diplomacy it is to <u>Listen</u>. By actively and truly listening we gain valuable information. As well as can pick up on real problems and underlying issues. So listen when seeking to resolve any issue. After that we have some more things to keep in mind while dealing with a conflict situation.

These attitudes are relevant whenever you want to advise, especially in a conflict which is not your own. It may be a friend telling you about a problem on the telephone. It may an informal chat with all conflicting parties. It may be a formally organized mediation session. Whatever the case may be, you want to practice the following:

Be Objective- Validate both sides, even if privately you prefer one point of view, or even when only one party is present. Address all points fairly. And seek to help other people see the validity of the point.

Be Supportive- Use caring language. Provide a non-threatening learning environment, where people will feel safe to open up. Say and show your understanding of a situation and/or point. Seek to use a calm tone, do not raise your voice unless you must (keep such brief). Seek to create an environment of calm and patience.

No Judging- Actively discourage judgments as to who was right and who was wrong. Don't ask "Why did you?" Ask "What happened?" and "How did you feel?" Do not allow people to influence events and make judgments of others. Seek to keep it more to feelings and facts. Steer the situation into an environment of sharing without fear of judgment.

Steer the Process, Not Content- Use astute questioning. Encouraging suggestions from participants. Resist advising. If your suggestions are really needed, offer as options not directives. Allow the process to work for you and those involved. Let the people involved come to conclusions and seek resolution; do not try to force it.

Win/Win- Work towards wins for both sides. Turn opponents into problem-solving partners. Look for solutions that benefit everyone involved. Seek to find compromises that work for all. Most often all will have to sacrifice something and likewise all should get something for it.

Ten Rules of Engagement (Fictional Jedi Conflict Rules) :
1. Let the Force be your guide.
2. Know your motives for becoming involved.
3. Seek to know the motives of others involved.
4. Be aware of outside motivators.
5. Understand the dark and light in all things.
6. Learn to see accurately.
7. Open your eyes to what is not evident.
8. Exercise caution, even in trivial matters.
9. Examine closely who benefits, and how they do so.
10. Examine closely who is harmed, and why.

::Section 3: L2 - Diplomacy Homework Assignment::
For One Week (Seven Days) observe your interactions with people. How many times did diplomacy come into play? How did you handle those situations? When you used diplomacy did you reach your desired outcome? What are the different ways which diplomacy comes into play?

Take the week to reflect and apply these principles. At the end of the week write your general thoughts and observations. I'll look to get a more interactive assignment up here eventually. Along with your general observations - diplomacy is about creative thinking. Thus solve this situation:
You are driving during a heavy storm, your car is packed with goods you are delivering to Red Cross relief efforts. You stop at a red light and notice at the bus stop your best friend waiting in the

weather. You pull over and notice also waiting at the bus stop is an old lady who looks to be sick and perhaps in need of medical attention. As well as your soulmate (insert dream boy/girlfriend here - even if you are currently with them) also waiting for the bus. The bus isn't due for another 15 minutes and due to the weather the bus may be late in arriving.

Due to your car being packed with goods you only have room to give one person a ride. What do you do? How do you best resolve the situation?

::MEDITATION::

Meditation, a subject in which many believe they know already. And why not? Many paths out there utilize a form of meditation. There are millions of books on the subject. Hundreds of Meditation retreat centers. The problem is usually information overload. Meditation is not so complex that it requires all of this. In fact, the essence of meditation just the opposite, simplification.

Jedi use meditation for a few specific reasons. And generally it is the purpose that governs which meditation technique one will use. Meditation done to cultivate a serene center is generally done in the morning, a breathing exercise combined with movement. Something akin to Qigong and Taijiquan. This is routinely done seeks to have long term affects.

Likewise if in the middle of work or school, we can get involved in heated situations, discussions, debates, or just buried by deadlines. In these times we do not have the luxury of taking a ten minute time-out, finding our center, and dealing with the issue at hand (though if you can do it, recommended). So instead we utilize some deep breaths, acknowledging how we feel, and calmly working towards the goal at hand. This simple a quick meditation is simply an exercise of acknowledgment, acceptance, control, and of course breathing.

These two different examples and two different approaches. Yet there are a plethora of techniques and ideas out there. Visualization methods, from simple 'imagine a peaceful place and go there' to full journeys that take you on a spiritual quest. Zazen is a popular method and requires little, except tons of practice. These contrast in style and even purpose, though the general desire is the same across the meditation board; to find peace within.

For the Jedi is there is little better than the simple act of stopping, breathing, and taking in life around you. Just stopping and smelling the roses, as it were. And the purpose is to appreciate life, to remind ourselves peace can be found in the chaos of life. Take a seat at a local Starbucks before the rush, and hang out until the morning rush is over. The hustle and bustle, the small worlds which briefly collide, and a world of stillness and peace (you).

Meditation need not be complex. The simple act of breathing is all that is required. And since that is something we have to do to survive anyhow, no special training required. At the same time, this is not meant to discourage the more involved techniques of meditation. Osho alone has many books on the wide variety of meditation techniques, from complex visualization to simple laughing in the mirror.

The main point here is enjoy meditation. It does not and should not be a chore. It is something we can bring into our daily lives in a variety of ways. And rather easy to practice on a daily basis. If you have meditations you enjoy, then continue to use them. Later one we will getting into specific meditation techniques both Jedi created and other meditations which Jed have found useful. For now you have the most basic technique from your Tier 1 practices.

::Section 3: L3 - Meditation Homework Assignment::

1.) As mentioned in the lecture. Find a popular place - local Starbucks or other coffee shop. Pick a day you have off. And go there during the morning rush. Seek to show up before the rush begins. And stay for a couple hours. Just take in life, observe, enjoy some tea or coffee, breathe, and just let life roll by. Bring a journal, notepad, et cetera, and jot down thoughts, observations, whatever comes to mind.

2.) Literally stop and smell the roses at some point. Getting ready for work, heading to the car, some roses near your porch? Just take a moment and appreciate the flowers. Take in the smell. You can change this up a bit according to what is available to you. But the main idea is to just stop when you normally wouldn't and appreciate beauty.

3.) After a week write your thoughts, observations, and insights.

Just reflect on the practices and what effect, if any, that it had. Also include any meditation techniques that you currently do regularly, if any.

_____
_____
_____
_____
_____
_____
_____
_____
_____
_____
_____
_____
_____
_____
_____
_____
_____
_____
_____
_____
_____
_____
_____
_____
_____
_____
_____
_____
_____
_____

::AWARENESS::

Awareness for a Jedi extends to all areas. Form physical surroundings to our own emotional motivations. Often times we can find that we are just drifting through life. Blissfully unaware of the happenings around us. We can, at times, get so caught up in our own little world, that we forget to think outside ourselves for even a moment. This can extend to simple things such as physical happenings around us, from not noticing the lamppost or chair, to not noticing someone's feelings or stance on a subject.

Awareness can play an important part in how we are able to react to various situations. A constant awareness is needed while driving. Through this we are able to avoid accidents and better adjust to the flow of traffic. A car slams on its brakes in front of us, but because we are aware of our surroundings we swiftly move into the lane knowing it is clear and we have room.

You are walking down to the store late at night, as you generally do. As you approach the store something feels off. You stop and look for a second to see if you can pick up on what it is. And you notice, the clerk isn't where he usually is, in fact the place look empty. That is odd, then you notice some of the products have been knocked over. As you are looking things over a person parks their car, jumps out, and heads right in, not giving a second thought. And bam, a person with a gun comes out of the backroom, grabs them, and takes that person to the backroom. You then take out your cellphone and call the local authorities. And again using your awareness and observation skills, you are able to pick up on what the gunman was wearing and give a description to the operator.

You are driving and suddenly traffic backs-up. As you take this route home all the time you know this to be unusual. Something must be up. As you get to an intersection you notice a car with its hazard lights on stuck in your lane. You go around and park your car, because you have noticed before a parking lot is just on the other side of the intersection and lights stay green for some time here. You jog back over to the intersection and when it turns green you help push the car to the parking lot and clear up traffic.

Awareness. Of our situation. Of our surroundings. Of our emotions. Of the emotions and beliefs of those around us. This is all part of being a Jedi. Understanding and taking into account where we are and who we are around. In this we give ourselves information to better act should we be call upon to do so.

Awareness plays a couple different roles within the Jedi Path. Awareness of self, awareness of others, awareness of motivations, awareness of our surroundings. We see awareness as a multi-layered aspect of the Jedi Path. Observation plays a part, paying attention plays a part, all of our senses play a part, including being aware of our intuition.

Thus awareness is not an easy thing to cultivate, because we have so many focal points. Remember that a Jedi must be aware of their surroundings and this includes online settings. The Force Academy allows us interaction with many different viewpoints in life. Thus being aware of where we post, what we are saying, and who will watching can really make a difference. Also, aware of our reactions, another person's motives, how we phrase our words, etc. As Jedi Awareness is a key part. And it helps out in so many different areas.

::Section 3: L4 - Awareness Homework Assignment::
A few exercises to practice over the Week:
1.) Play the -What is Different- Game. With just about everyone you see seek to pick out something that sets them apart from others. Shoes untied, muttering to themselves, shirt is inside-out, walks with their head completely down, cellphone worn on left-side of belt, et cetera.
2.) Take a moment and try to take in as much as you can without looking around. Just take in the big picture. Just take your surroundings with that wide field of vision. And if able, take a mental snapshot, close your eyes, and see what you can recall

from the center outwards. Easier to do when alone and with sunglasses as a tip. And no practicing while driving.

3.) Take note of your surroundings in general. Maybe play the -What If- Game; what if a car drove off the road right now, what would I do, where could I go. What if a gunman came in right now, what could I do, where could I go? Exits? Open lane in traffic? Closest Off-ramp? Windows, Doors, type of people. Just note where you are, whats around you, who is around, and if able or in need entertain yourself if scenarios and solutions.

Practice, Reflection, Thoughts.

_____
_____
_____
_____
_____
_____
_____
_____
_____
_____
_____
_____
_____
_____
_____
_____
_____
_____
_____
_____
_____
_____

::PHYSICAL FITNESS::

Physical Well-Being, this is the concept of physical fitness. For the Jedi this is a broad idea. Covering concepts such as healthy immune system, healthy mind healthy body harmony, being physically capable of helping out in situations, promoting longer life, so on and so forth. And there are many, many ways to achieve this goal of fitness.

From practice of various martial arts, standard running and healthy diet routine, P90X, hiking, yoga, the list is long and varied. Here at the Jedi Foundation we encourage certain practices and exercises. We have our own system of work-out routines and self-defense training. But we encourage any system that works and provides results to the individual.

After all, we cannot force you to put down the twinkie and pick up the apple. We are not all in a position to switch to organic food, lets face it, that can be an expensive life choice. Process food is often cheaper. We cannot wake you up in the morning like a Drill Sergeant and run you through a work-out routine. Thus you have to find what works with you, your lifestyle, your schedule, and provides good results.

The fact is, you are going to have to sacrifice some of your time to find results. This isn't about losing weight, this isn't about the latest craze in quick diet results. We are talking overall, long term health, which does require life long practice. So we are going to provide some tips here to help you get started on your physical fitness.

::Training::
Warm Up First. Get the blood flowing, the muscles stretched. Take it slow. Train form over speed and repetition. Gain control and stability first.
Stretch when you wake-up. Stretch when you go to bed. Keep the body limber.

::Diet::

Seek to use organic foods rather then processed foods. Plenty of resources available on that.

Water - A must. Stay hydrated: 8 to 10 glasses a day. Do not seek to exceed a gallon. And for every soda you drink, drink a glass of water (my personal rule).

More Meals - Less Food. Look to have six small "meals" a day. Snack it up on trail mix. Look up small meal plans for ideas on what you can do to change your eating habits.

Fruit after work-outs often provide the best source with their simple sugars.

Try not to eat an hour before working out or before sleeping. Let the food work for you.

Easy on the Alcohol. A glass of red wine with dinner, not bad. A bottle? Bad. There are some benefits to alcohol consumption, however it requires extreme moderation. Your body doesn't require it - so feel free to avoid it all together.

::Healthy Mind::

It worked as a kid - Feel free to grab that nap. Can go a long away to breaking up the day and providing plenty of energy to tackle all you have to handle in the day. Just be sure to set the alarm.

Seek to get a full nights rest. A continuous sleep cycle works best - so make sure you are comfortable and have a mind ready for rest.

Meditation - not only can it help ease the mind for bed, but also let go of stress. Stress is horrible for the body.

Schedule helps regulate the body. Seek to have a constant sleep schedule as best as you can.

::General::

Get some Sun. Seek to make it a goal to get 10 to 15 minutes of direct sunlight. Get out there and breathe some fresh air. Maybe some meditation practice in the afternoon.

Smoking has no benefits. Free radical damage, lung damage,

smells horrible on clothes. Seek to cut it out.

Shower after working out. Not only as a courtesy to those around you - it removes toxins and promotes healthy skin.

::Section 3: L5 - Physical Fitness Homework Assignment::

Take a day to reflect on your normal/average fitness habits (diet, exercise routine, sleeping habits, etc.). And not only reflect on those habits, but observe them throughout the day. Next day see where you might be able to improve. Or areas you'd like to improve but aren't currently able (e.g. parents control the food budget and aren't going organic), yet still look for small changes you can make. How can you improve your overall fitness? Set about doing that, making those changes. You have a week to research various ways and tips to improve upon your fitness. After the week is up, just update with your thoughts, changes, and any experiences or insights.

_____

_____

_____

_____

_____

_____

_____

_____

_____

_____

_____

_____

_____

_____

_____

_____

_____

_____

SECTION FOUR: THE FIVE TRAITS -

::PATIENCE::

There is no bigger tool to the Jedi than patience. Patience serves a Jedi very well in all manner of practices and situations. First as Jedi we need to understand that nothing is going to come to us over night. We will not wake-up one morning and find out we are Jedi Masters, not without plenty of time and training of course. Thus patience proves us the ability to see our training through the rest of our lives.

Patience also applies to just about every trait one can associate with the Jedi. When we think of diplomacy, emotional control, self-discipline, peace, serenity, learning, teaching, et cetera we can see the value of patience within these things. Each one will require a Jedi to be patient and to exercise that patience more than once.

Patience can seem hard to develop, falls under the same issue as Self-discipline. It is not truly something that can be taught our passed on, merely something explained and practiced daily. This presents a challenge to Jedi Hopefuls, as they are in complete control of themselves and their training. Will you seek to develop patience daily? Or will you simply allow yourself excuses and rationalize your inaction?

To help develop patience one should seek not only to practice it daily, but to consciously practice it daily. You may notice how much you patience you have already, quietly waiting for a stoplight, calmly waiting for someone to figure out a solution to a problem you know inside and out. Two major things I recommend for developing patience is breathing deeply at times when you feel impatient. Like when you are late for work or school and you hit every red light. Or when someone just isn't getting what you are explaining to them. Breath deeply and be patient. Another thing to try is to make yourself do nothing. Sit in front of a clock, no music, no movies, no games, no books, nothing but you and a clock. Sit quietly for 5 to 10 minutes. Develop the ability to sit quietly for extended periods of time, this will help.

Patience by: Jedi Trad Davin

Patience is a virtue all Jedi should learn; I cannot stress this enough. It is one of the first things you will learn, and one of the most important. If a Jedi is not patient, with his studies and with others, then the pull of the Dark Side increases. You want things quicker and easier, which is the way of the Dark Side.

Many a Jedi have fallen because they believe that their Master is not teaching them as much as they need. They believe they are ready for more knowledge and tests, when in reality they forsake the most important lessons. You must work diligently on the lessons your Master gives you. Explore, learn, and discover every facet of the lesson; master it. Continue to do this through-out your training. You will be presented with more lessons as the time presents itself.

A Jedi must also be patient with others. Let us use an example: You are on a basketball, or football team. The coach is giving you a new play. It seems simple to you; you quickly learn it and perform it well.

There is another player on the team who cannot get it. Every time you run through the play he makes a mistake- he just cannot seem to learn it. Now, you have a choice. You may choose to be angry with him and yell at him for not getting it right. Or, you may be patient with him, and try to help him understand it. I suggest you choose the latter. This way he'll probably understand it, you won't be angry, and you will have learned patience. Not to mention that the play will probably work better.

You see, if you are patient with others, they will have a higher respect for you and a better opinion of you. You will have more friends, and strong friendships. You will also see things from their point of view, and you can benefit others. They can also help you on troubles you have. This begins to teach other virtues: Unity and teamwork.

Be patient in every thing you do. If you watch the Jedi in the Star Wars movies, you will notice that while they might start out reckless (ie. young Obi-Wan and Luke in ESB), they eventually learn patience. They are cool headed and able to think clearly in dangerous situations. This is always a plus. So learn patience, practice it, and test yourself in real-life situations. Remind yourself to be patient always. This is the way of the Light Side, and of a true Jedi. ***

This is a core element of the Jedi and one that is tested the most. In everything we do patience is required, sometimes we must be patient with others, at other times we must be patient with circumstances, and one of the hardest is to be patient with ourselves. This is the lot of a Jedi Knight, being able to take a deep breath, step back and re-approach the situation as needed. Emotional Control, Inner Peace, Tolerance of Others, Acceptance of loss, over-coming pain, all these things require patience. And without it, you will never make it as a Jedi.

So how does one cultivate patience? This is not an easy thing, and yet once attained it seems easy enough to achieve. Patience is usually just a matter of taking a mere second to reflect on the issue at hand. To ask an important question of yourself or of a situation; example being when you find yourself in a argument that seems to be getting out of control. Take a moment and just ask, why are emotions running high? Why do I need to raise my voice? How can I make my point without offending the other person? Understand that any situation can be handled with an objective mind and a calm demeanor.

Do not allow yourself to be swept away in the heat of the moment. In this you will find that you can wait through a lot of things. Yet this focuses more on patience with others. Others times you need patience within yourself. Such as waiting for the cable man to arrive who is taking his sweet time. An easy patience to cultivate patience is to focus your mind. Meditation is a great way to calm and focus your mind and do something positive with your time. Just take a moment to close your eyes and focus on your breathing. Allow the worries and cares of the world to drift away for a few minutes, knowing you will come back to them later and resolve them. Just relax, breathe, and allow time to continue its flow as you cultivate a peaceful mind and new energy.

In our world it may seem like the world will not wait for us. Bills are due on a certain date, exams will not be delayed, and dinner will get cold if left alone. Internet moves at high speed, freeway (highway) speed limits have increased, our world is just moving at a faster pace these days. Yet that does not mean we have to always move at that pace. Patience is sitting calmly at a Red Light, even though you are running late. It is in the waiting of a person who is late for an appointment, understanding that several things could have held them up. Or the waiting for a package to arrive even though you could really use what your ordered already. Or in the long process of becoming a Jedi Knight when you have only just begun your training.

Be Patient, be mindful, and accept that things will happen in their own course of time. Not all lessons can be taught by lectures or assignments, some things must be learned in time and as a Jedi you must allow for that time. Many things can help with your patience, meditation, a good book, a re-reading of lessons like this one, or any lesson which relates to the Jedi.

::Section 4: L1 - Patience::

Exercise your patience. Observe, be mindful of times when you become rushed and/or impatient. Whether you are late for work, school, appointment and things keep slowing you up. Or when you feel you have to explain something very simple to someone for the fifth time. Keep this observation going for one week, it is recommended that you keep a record, perhaps a journal to log the times you notice/remember when you lost your patience.

Also during this time seek to work on your patience. Use

Time; Take a second, just take a deep breath, close your eyes, breathe, relax, and now approach your task. Use Logic; if rushing makes one careless, does it really save time? By taking the extra seconds to just breathe and handle things in a more controlled manner you may save more than time. Many accidents are caused by people rushing. And remember, no one is perfect, so allow for mistakes both for others and definitely for yourself.

::OBJECTIVITY::

Objective thinking, there is simply no other way for a Jedi. A Jedi must take all sides into account, giving each person a fair hearing, and allow for all possibilities to exist. Bias, emotions, desire, these cannot be allowed to affect a Jedi's judgment. A Jedi must remain a fair neutral party in all that they do. By doing so they establish themselves as a Jedi (and order) that prizes justice, honesty, fairness, and objectiveness above all other things. Whether they like a person or not, whether they know the person is guilty for something else or not, if they are not the issue of the situation than they are not the issues which a Jedi focuses on.

In any situation people must be able to understand that a Jedi acts and bases their judgment upon clear logical facts and evidence. They are completely impartial, acting in a objective manner to bring a mutual resolution to the table. Adhering to local customs and laws and not allowing their own feelings and beliefs to interfere with any justice process.

One must understand that a Jedi's decisions are not based upon friendship or desire. Thus should a Jedi act against his friend, or disagree with him, it is important to note that it is nothing personal. It is simply logical fact which leads a Jedi to their conclusions. In this a Jedi is free to remove themselves from judgments and situations which have a conflict of interest. That is fair and objective as well. A Jedi must know when their presence and even judgment might compromise the validity and fairness of any given situation.

Another form of objective thinking is considering action. A Jedi has to accept that there is more than one outcome to a situation. They have to plan for success, failure, allies, opponents, and the many roads in between. Keeping a clear and open mind to the many possibilities that exist in any situation. A Jedi may take action, but also be prepared for the action to have many different consequences. If a Jedi merely thinks that they will walk into a situation and be able to resolve it, they are not thinking objectively and have already started to fail.

Evidence, facts, logic, reason, and listening to all parties in involved. Accepting the many outcomes of a situation, success, failure, and the variations. These are the keys to objective thinking. And yet this must also be applied to the Jedi themselves. A Jedi must be objective and honest with themselves if they expect to grow. They cannot believe themselves better than others or inferior to others just because. They must address themselves as everything else, looking at evidence, facts, and opinions. It is than that a Jedi can truly grow and strengthen their weaknesses.

::Section 4: L2 - Objectivity Homework Assignment::
Take an objective look back at your training (thus far), your time here, and most importantly at yourself. Give a detailed objective look at your growth, your strengths, and your weaknesses. Also an objective guideline as to how to overcome your weaknesses, if you demand it necessary.

_____

_____

_____

_____

_____

_____

_____

_____

_____

_____

_____

_____

_____

_____

_____

_____

_____

::RELIABILITY::

Jedi are reliable, but what does this really mean? Does this mean a Jedi never fails, is never wrong, or never has to call in sick to work/school? Simply put it means one can rely on a Jedi to be a Jedi. Jedi are indeed trustworthy and reliable, but they do make mistakes, they do fail, and they are able to get sick. Yet when they call into school or work it is because they fully believe they would be more of a problem than an asset.

Jedi can be relied upon to be Jedi. Another circular phrase, which deserves a bit of explanation. Jedi, as we have seen hold to peace, knowledge, serenity, harmony, and the Force. And one can count on a Jedi to keep these core values close. Personally healthy, diplomatic, calm in stressful situations, these things are what Jedi are. And when one talks to an actual Jedi we can rely on the Jedi to be a model of these things and more. It is merely who Jedi are, what they represent.

Reliability for a Jedi comes in the fashion of Jedi keeping their word. A Jedi should promise little yet at the same deliver much more, as much as possible. In this a Jedi will be able to uphold their promises and set that standard of dependability, reliability. If a Jedi promises they will do something than they should do that and seek to go a step beyond. Again though you have to use common sense, in all duties, even charities, there are lines and boundaries. A Jedi should respect when doing more than requested would be a violation of trust or responsibility.

Also a Jedi must be relied upon to say no. A Jedi is not a doormat, a Jedi is not a slave, a Jedi is not a get out of work free card. People must rely on the Jedi to do what is necessary and trust they will back off when it is appropriate. A Jedi helps others, to help themselves. No individual, group, organization, or even government should ever come to depend solely on the Jedi. They must rely on the Jedi to help them (either an individual, group, organization, or government) become more capable and grow themselves. Jedi are not the means to an end, they are bridge to help others reach the end themselves.

::Section 4: L3 - Reliability Homework Assignment::

Take a week to observe and apply this trait. At the end of the week answer these questions:
In what ways are you reliable? How can you or have you made yourself more reliable? Does being having others rely on you make you a slave and/or a weaker individual? Does it make the person(s) relying on you weak or weaker? Explain your answers.

_____

_____

_____

_____

_____

_____

_____

_____

_____

_____

_____

_____

_____

_____

_____

_____

_____

_____

_____

_____

_____

_____

_____

_____

::HUMILITY::

Humility, has more than one meaning in relation to the Jedi. Many feel this relates simply that a Jedi does not act arrogant, self-centered, and instead lowers him/herself to stay on the same level as everyone around them. Yet this is not exactly correct. A simple fact is that the more your train to better yourself the more better you become over those that do not. This is simply how it works, those that work towards self-betterment become better. Knowing this is not arrogance, it is self-awareness, self-knowledge. A Jedi is better than others, because they train to be.

How does this relate to humility? So what, that is basically what it comes down to. So a Jedi is better, a Jedi understand that does not hive him/her special privileges. Better, but still with the same friends, still eats, wears clothes, bleeds when cut. A Jedi understands that self-betterment is not a ticket to special rights, honors, or privileges. So they continue to do what they do. They do the best they can in all they do. But they are not in it to gloat, to have the ego-stroked, to gain praise. They help those who request it based upon logic, not skin color, religion, belief, et cetera. A Jedi is not looking to place themselves above others, they recognize that anyone can be as good as them if they merely trained to be. It is merely matter of training.

On that token no one is born into Jedihood. No one wakes up and suddenly finds themselves a Jedi. It is something trained for, something lived by. And all Jedi start out on the bottom. I knew a kid who was picked on, not liked such in school. Self-esteem issues were a big problem when he started training. After training for about a year he noticed he was stronger physically, he was smarter, more aware of facts, and logical deduction. He was capable of defending himself, he was more aware of his surroundings, he was walking with his head up for a change, and he was clever form his studies and readings.

This had an effect. He started saying the things he was

95

thinking. He started calling people on their lies. And every person that pushed in, he pushed back (no matter which way they pushed, physically, emotionally, mentally). He was empowered, he realized he had capabilities above those around him, he saw things much quicker than others. He could read situations and people and thus was able to alter situations to play out how he desired.

This of course becomes a selfish thing. Striking back at those that struck at you once. Allowing fights, embarrassing people. Showing everyone you are the best there is, inflating your ego that had been bruised so many times before. It is not about justice, but simply ego, retribution, striking back. Humility comes in play here. Humility counteracts the ego, humility allows us to be better without the need to travel down a path of retribution.

As that young Jedi learned, a Jedi does not need to prove anything. And doing so only leads to what many would call the dark side. Indulging in selfish desire and outcomes, hurting others to prove your self better. This is simply not the Jedi Way. And by accepting our abilities and using them to better help others help themselves we accept our role in society. We are not lawmakers, we are not law enforcement, we simply are individuals we have trained hard and use those skills to help others along their own path.

Better? Most likely. What does that amount to? Merely how much we are able to help and support others. And this is the main focus of the Jedi, we better ourselves so that we may be in a better position to help others help themselves. The only reason we are better is because we took the time to better ourselves and someone took the time to help us in that goal. Remember we did not become Jedi simply because we are that good, but because many help us along the way.

::Section 4: L4 - Humility Homework Assignment::
Take a week to observe and apply this trait. At the end of the week answer these questions:
Does Humility mean denying or even lying about your abilities?

In what ways can a Jedi humble themselves? List a moment in your own life in which humility served you best. Explain your answers.

_____
_____
_____
_____
_____
_____
_____
_____
_____
_____
_____
_____
_____
_____
_____
_____
_____
_____
_____
_____
_____
_____
_____
_____
_____
_____
_____
_____
_____
_____
_____

::WISDOM::

While Jedi seek to preserve of knowledge, they understand that it takes wisdom to use knowledge properly. While Jedi are seen as wise, they merely work from knowledge, experience, and the Force. Wisdom we can say is the combination of knowledge + experience.

A Jedi gains wisdom and knowledge by being mindful; mindful of themselves, their surroundings, environment, feelings, and how all things these tend to link together. Where we live, who we hang out with, our family, all things things have an effect on us. As Jedi we must be aware of this and seek to overcome the hurdles in our lives.

In our experience in life we gain the wisdom of life. Likewise as we progress as Jedi we gain wisdom into the Jedi lifestyle. Wisdom is a fancy and overrated way of saying "been there, done that." Truly wisdom is simply the combination of our accumulated knowledge and our experiences with said knowledge.

It is said that wisdom is to know something deeply. To be enlightened about a certain subject (whether that subject be life or automobiles). It is one thing to know that placing your hand in a fire will hurt. It is another to know the exact process, exactly what happens and what it does. In this wisdom you know how to avoid it. *"I have to place my hand in the fire to grab that ring. I know via knowledge and experience that if I drench my hand in water that I have more time without being burned. I know via knowledge and experience my long sleeves will catch fire so I'll remove those. I know via knowledge and experience that metal ring will be extremely hot and will need to hold it with something."* In this you can create the best approach to retrieving the ring from the fire. And one watching may praise your wisdom in the matter.

This is what it means to be wise as a Jedi. That you have

studied, you have trained, you have observed, you have experienced (even gained the experience of others), and are able to consider the most possible scenarios in the least possible time, with the best possible outcomes/options. And the more you exercise this the more wisdom you gain from it (even in mistakes and failures). The more you work on wisdom the more you gain it.

Wisdom comes to us everyday. From knowing the best ways to get to work/school, to how best to deal with a friend in any given situation. We can rely on our own personal skills/abilities, our knowledge of the situation, and our previous experiences to get us through. And when we lack in one f those, it is rather easy correct. And in the end, by just taking that leap forward we can be sure we will gain the wisdom for the next time (or how to avoid a next time).

::Section 4: L5 - Wisdom Homework Assignment::
Take a week to observe and apply this trait. At the end of the week answer these questions:
How can a Jedi seek to gain wisdom? Are Jedi automatically wise (meaning if you are a Jedi does that make you wise by simply being a Jedi?) How does wisdom play a role in a Jedi's life? Explain your answers.

_____

_____

_____

_____

_____

_____

_____

_____

_____

_____

_____

_____

SECTION FIVE: THE FIVE TRUTHS -

::SELF-HONESTY::

Honesty is an important thing, but as individuals we need to focus a lot more on self-honesty first. Does this mean forgo being honest with others? No, just means as a Jedi you need to really come to terms with yourself first. You must be brutally honest with yourself, your weaknesses, your strengths, your mistakes, regrets, your successes and failures. And honestly, this is where most Jedi fail. It is hard to look at your life objectively and not want to throw it all away right there. Or maybe that is just me.

Fact is that Jedi must be completely aware of themselves, their motives, their feelings, their abilities, they must know what exactly they are capable of. And this knowledge only come with being brutally honest with yourself. That honest should extend outward, but Jedi understand that sometimes the truth is not needed. We will address that soon enough, but for now I want to really stress that importance of knowing yourself. It is easy to fluff this off, to say you already know everything you need to know about yourself. You are afraid of spiders, you are a quick learner, you enjoy traveling, so on and so forth. But is this really you? How far does that knowledge extend? How far are you willing to go to save a complete stranger? What will you do if someone just starts punching you while you are standing in line at the grocery store? Lost in a blizzard?

What are your limits, physical, mental, and otherwise? What won't you do, just won't do it. What will break you? What inspires you? Why do you react that way? Why do you feel a certain way during a rainy day? You have to really examine and be honest with yourself. These answers and the deeper meaning in them are for no one but yourself. Only one person needs to truly know you, inside and out, and that is you. Lie to others if you must, but be completely open and honest with yourself. You are not fat because of some gene, you are fat because you love cheeseburgers and never work-out or go running. Honesty first Jedi.

That being said how does honesty relate outside the self? As Jedi we understand we must be brutally honest with ourselves, but what about others. As I said before, sometimes the truth is not needed. This does not mean you are open to lie all the time for no reason, but at times a Jedi understands that allowing people to believe their own misinformation and/or half-truths is best. I cannot give specific examples, but I have no doubt that we can all think of personal experiences in which we knew it was best to keep the truth to ourselves and allow others to believe what they want to believe. Whether that is something as simple as the old "Honey do I look fat in this?" 📄 or something a bit more in-depth, there are times when it is best to allow others to form their own conclusions.

A Jedi does not seek to outwardly deceive, they are not looking to lie or mislead anyone. Honestly there is not a whole lot of reason to. Seek to spread open honesty by practicing it yourself. Sometimes there s nothing one can say, but allow each person to make of the truth what they will. Offer the truth, if they cannot handle it, that is their choice. As a Jedi you are the avatar of the Force, your actions reflect on all Jedi and the Force; lies and deceit are not core to either of these, so do not make them common practice.

Know thy self, in order to accomplish that self-honesty is needed. It is only than we can extend that honesty to others.

::Section 5: L1 - Self-Honesty Homework Assignment::

Take a week to seek and develop honesty within yourself and outwardly. Look at the various situations you find yourself in over the week. By the end of the week pick a situation to report on (though all situations should have the following questions in

103

mind) -

What is/was the situation?

Ask yourself (and answer in the report):

What is the truth here?

Am I avoiding the truth here?

Is a desire for money, power, respect, or acceptance, clouding the truth?

Is a fear of confrontation, pain, loneliness, death or the unknown clouding the truth?

Am I honestly scanning myself to recognize the truth here, am I honestly listening to it even if I don't like what it says? Or is my pride, or my fear, or other ego and emotional blocks in the way?

_____

_____

_____

_____

_____

_____

_____

_____

_____

_____

_____

_____

_____

_____

_____

_____

_____

_____

_____

_____

_____

::LEARNING::

A Jedi is an eternal student. There is no stopping in the learning process for a Jedi. This comes in a variety of ways. In life we often get a chance to learn new things. Whether that is starting a new job and learning new skills with it. Or a new hobby and having a more experienced person show us more about it. Or when life presents us with a new situation we have never faced before. And in all of these whether we succeed or not does not determine our ability to learn. Often times we learn more from our mistakes than our successes.

For a Jedi we must not approach things with our own ideas, our own assumptions. We may be well-versed in a hobby or subject, yet by listening and being the student to others within that area we can gain new perspectives (agreed with or not) and new ideas. We can find ways not to do things as well as improve how we already do things. The amount of information in any given subject is often rather larger. And taking the time (putting aside the ego) to understand another person's experience and take on something can really prove to be very useful (in a number of ways).

It is here that we might say a Jedi carries with them the beginner's mind. They approach things with a fresh perspective seeking to gain as much as possible from the subject and those willing to share their own experiences and lessons within any given subject.

It is important that we allow the experience of others to be a guide. There are always times we will want to verify something. Confirm it with our own experiences. However that should only be done after serious thought and logical reflection. The experience of those who came before us can be extremely helpful and relevant. As much as we like to think we know better, there is no denying the benefit of experience (whether you or someone else).

As Jedi we must be willing to really listen and consider the advise and experiences of others, especially those who have already gone through such situations before. IN this we can navigate life much easier. By learning history we can avoid repeats. This holds for personal history as well. Learning how a person failed on several jobs interviews can help you avoid those pitfalls. And sometimes that is the best advise, not how to do something, but simply what to avoid.

"I won't tell you how to perform your job interview, but I can tell you what to avoid as it cost me the interview. First dressing as you would to hang out with friends does not help, no matter the job. Second, don't comment on the interviewer's spouse. Got me in trouble more than once..." You get the idea, sometimes the best lessons we need to learn are avoiding pitfalls. But we must we willing to give and take advice. This comes with humbling ourselves, being able to listen when we think we know better.

Remember - Jedi take the time to learn. For one never knows when useless knowledge will become life saving knowledge.

::Section 5: L2 - Learning Homework Assignment::
Describe a situation/subject you had to learn recently. Whether it be in school, a new job, new hobby, etc. Do you feel you took the time to properly learn it? What was your approach to learning it (asking advise from more experienced individuals, trial and error, book study)? Do you feel if given the chance you would try to approach it differently now, try to learn a different way? Why or why not?

_____
_____
_____
_____
_____
_____

::GUIDANCE::

Last week we looked at learning and how a Jedi seeks to approach things with a beginner's mind. They humble themselves so that they may benefit from the experience and knowledge of others. The flip-side to that is a Jedi ends up gaining a bit of experience and knowledge themselves. They start to accumulate wisdom through the various learning, knowledge, and experience they go through. That wisdom may benefit a Jedi many times throughout their life, but it won't serve that many if simply kept to the self.

Jedi are not selfish individuals. They do not seek to gain wisdom and knowledge for themselves alone. They gain it so that they may better help others. So that they may help guide others down a more gentler path. A Jedi takes the wealth of knowledge and experience they have gained and seek to pass it on so that others may use it. And it is not for the Jedi to decision when it gets used.

There are pieces of advice and lessons in my head given to me at a young age. I ignored them and suffered the consequences of that decision. Yet later in life those words come back to us and we avoid the danger. Sometimes we are given advice we do not believe has anything to do with us and than 5 years later that advice saves our bacon. And Jedi understands that we have to remove our ego from guiding others, just as we need to when learning.

Someone may not get what we are telling them because they are not ready to accept such truths. And that is fine. People are free to make their own mistakes. We cannot force people to come to a conclusion, because that will never last. The most lastly change is the change sought out by choice. The person must come to the decision on their own. And we must humbly accept that we are simply a signpost. We cannot make a person turn left, we can simply and clearly state that left will get them to their desired destination.

This is how a Jedi guides. They present the options, they offer advice, they share their own experiences, they give lessons, and lectures on situation at hand. And than they let go and hope that the advice and guidance helps the person choose the proper and less painful path in life. A Jedi also recognizes and points out that what works for one may not work for another. We all have individuals needs, wants, and desires, which add to our uniqueness. Yet we are all human, and we all fall into similar traps in life. By-product of all of us having human-nature.

So a Jedi recognizes the uniqueness of every situation,a s well as points out the inherent similarities in all situations. And through our own lessons, the lessons of others, and the knowledge of the people and situation at hand a Jedi offers guidance. They assume the signpost position and offer direction. And then they wait, ready to be that signpost again, since most people won't listen until after-the-fact.

A Jedi guides by being an example. That is the best way, it gives you something to point to, to show for taking your advice. A Jedi is an example, they are a signpost, and they are there again and again. It is sink or swim all the time, a Jedi can offer help, but a Jedi should not do all the heavy lifting. People should always be encouraged to live their own life, a Jedi should empower others to follow their own ideals, not rely on the Jedi all the time.

Sometimes a Jedi must step in, sometimes a Jedi must let go, and sometimes a Jedi needs to simply stay right in the middle. How will you know? That is something you are going to have to discover yourself. Each person and situation is different. Trust your feelings within the situation and follow the Jedi Method. And learn and grow from whatever the outcome may be.

::Section 5: L3 - Guidance Homework Assignment::
Just take the week to reflect on this. Observe in that time situations in which you are the guide, when you are giving the lesson, and offering the guidance to others. What lessons in regards to Guidance did you learn from it? Also what are your

general thoughts on guidance and the part it plays in the Jedi
lifestyle?

_____

_____

_____

_____

_____

_____

_____

_____

_____

_____

_____

_____

_____

_____

_____

_____

_____

_____

_____

_____

_____

_____

_____

_____

_____

_____

_____

_____

111

::SACRIFICE::

"Our way is that of a series of difficult choices." - Jedi Eng Cabot

As a Jedi you are expected to be in control. That means in the middle of a highly emotional situation you are to remain in control of your emotions and actions (reactions). And that does mean bottling up emotion for a short period of time - You will feel fear, anger, rage, sorrow, love, hate, happiness, sadness, and you must still act/react as a Jedi. Acting from a place of objectivity, serenity, and mindfulness. You will expected to put the needs of others above yourself. You will be expected to deal with your emotions in a healthy manner, just because you put them aside to deal with something does not mean you have dealt with them.

As a Jedi there needs to be the continual balance of mind and body. Healthy body, eating right, staying fit, as well as keeping the mind sharp and developing the powers of the brain (diplomacy, literacy, logic, etc.). The reality of being a Jedi is that there is a lot of study, training, and boring aspects to be placed on top of the duties of the Path. And no cool Jedi Master to make sure you do it.

We can look at these things individually and see what we are giving up. We give-up a lot of freedoms people take for granted. The freedom to slap someone in the face for being an @$$hole. The right to snap and yell and insult people right back who are unjustly attacking us or others. As Jedi we must retain that control of ourselves to simply act. We know and recognize the consequences of our actions, and thus we are held to a higher standard. We are held to a way to resolve things without giving into our emotional nature.

Personal relationships love to thrive off emotional imbalance. And sometimes family, lovers, even friends will do all they can to push our buttons simply because they want to have that emotional response. It is not that we are cold unfeeling robots, we can very much show love, care, and tenderness to those we care about. But in our search for inner peace and especially in obtaining inner peace, that often (almost always) manifests outwardly as well. And thus we tend to remain calm more often than not and that can bother people. Especially in a society that seems so focused on "drama" as a way of life at the moment.

Another form of sacrifice that Jedi often experience is giving of themselves, their time, and even their resources (money, etc.). Jedi seek to help others and even in helping them to help themselves a Jedi must give in order to see change. And because of this a Jedi will shoulder a lot of responsibility. A Jedi is faced with the same problems we see fictional superheroes faced with. Peter Parker is a great fictional example of a person conflicted between trying to lead a normal (what everyone expects life) and the responsibilities that have fallen to him. It is a tough struggle that does not always result in the ending we want.

A Jedi accepts that there will be times between choosing a personal desire and choosing the helpful (the Jedi) option. And all we can do is hope that people in our lives understand our decision to try and make the world a bit better. And that does mean sometimes you will have to choose others over them. We give ourselves, we give our emotional strength, spiritual strength, physical strength, our time, money, knowledge, experiences. We put ourselves out there in hopes that others will see that, learn form it, and return it even just a little. And in being examples and people returning it, the world starts to get back into the idea that if we work for the greater whole we automatically are working for ourselves. We can put the needs of the many and the needs of the few in the exact same category (choice), but we have to get their first and that requires a lot of work and unfortunately personal sacrifice.

The Jedi Life has its drawbacks, it is a life of sacrifice. And if you have a dream and the Jedi Lifestyle will compromise that dream, or somehow destroy that dream, than feel free to follow your heart. You need not sacrifice your own happiness for this path. The lucky few of us, our dream is to be a Jedi. As such we are open (and limited by Jedi Ideals) to any career that we may find a calling in. And we know Jedi can be used everywhere from Retail to Government Workers (DMV, IRS, International equivalents).

What you need to understand is that the Jedi Path does have restrictions. But they should never stop you from experiencing and enjoying life. In fact they should help you not only enjoy such moments more, but also help keep others safe to also enjoy them. Sometimes we seem the downers, but really we want people to fully experience life and have the opportunity to have many more experiences. In this we often get the chance to show a new way of experiencing, giving a couple options to an otherwise tunnel-visioned individual.

But I digress; the point is that you are and always should be a Jedi because that is how you want to live your life. You have looked at life, the many ways to live it, and have made the decision that the Jedi Way is simply the best way for you to live your life.

We see sacrifice is a part of our path. We see restrictions within our path. This is simply part of being a Jedi. Do not make those sacrifices, do not set yourself back, do not shoulder the burdens if this is not for you. Jedi accept the sacrifices we make because we believe in the greater good that comes from it. We see the benefit of those sacrifices, but they only make sense within the Jedi Path. To make such sacrifices just because? That would just be silly.

I leave on this old quote:

"This is important to understand as a Jedi, as few decisions we make do not involve sacrifice. What comes with training and experience is the courage and conviction to make the cut, as well as the wisdom of knowing where to cut. Preservation of life is the way of the Force, and choosing the best way to do this is the way of the Jedi." - Jedi Baal Legato

::Section 5: L4 - Sacrifice Homework Assignment::

I want you to take the week to reflect and observe. When often have you been called on to sacrifice of yourself in order to help and guide others? (feel free to share examples of sacrifices you have made) Do you feel that such sacrifice is worth it? Do you believe a Jedi should <u>always </u>sacrifice themselves (consider it carefully)? Why or Why not?

_____
_____
_____
_____
_____
_____
_____
_____
_____
_____
_____
_____
_____
_____
_____
_____
_____
_____
_____
_____
_____
_____
_____
_____

::COMMITMENT::

A Jedi cannot be a Jedi without commitment. It is a lifelong pursuit and one that will not happen overnight. Jedi train for years before reaching the accepted level of Jedi Knight. And even than it is continuation to the Jedi Path that helps one progress. Self-discipline helps a Jedi complete their training and sees them through as they live as Jedi. Yet it is Commitment, that dedication to the Jedi Path that keeps them going for the rest of their lives.

As it has been said many times, being a Jedi is not easy. It will test every single person that walks its' path. Why keep going? Because we have committed ourselves to the Jedi Way (to something greater than ourselves), we are dedicated to live as Jedi every day of our lives. It is in this that commitment plays its part. When tested by life, friends, loved ones, bosses, teachers, governments, we will find are ourselves asking why. And in these moments we can see the benefit of walking away from the Jedi Path.

But by having commitment we give ourselves that time to take that second look. We give ourselves the time to exercise patience and look at things with a calm, clear, logical mind. And it is than we must decide whether or not we should continue walking the Jedi Path. Emotions can run life, stress can stretch us thin, and it is in these times that we must rely on our commit to the Jedi, their ideals, and philosophies, before we make any rash decisions.

Commitment is not something taught. It is a question of why you sought to become a Jedi in the first place. Do you have the dedication to see this through to the end? I cannot pass on my commitment to the Jedi, it is something that will always be in me. The question you have to ask yourself is whether or not you are committed to living as a Jedi every single day? Knowing it is not the easiest path to walk. Such commitment is going to be tested.

And while I wish I could just pass on a secret to sticking it out, there is only you and your desire to be a Jedi.

You have shown commitment by reaching this far. It has been a long road simply to reach this point. And yet a longer road awaits. And an even longer one after that. And so it goes with the Jedi, it is never over. We continue forward step-by-step. And it is our own dedication, our own commitment that allows us to continue to help others in the way we believe works for the greatest good. We believe the Jedi Path is worth following and thus we commit ourselves to pursuing it and perfecting it. This brings us one step closer to honoring the inspiration that brought us here, to being full Jedi. And the only thing that will keep us on that road is our personal commitment to the path.

::Section 5: L5 - Commitment Homework Assignment::
I feel commitment to anything should be recognized and rewarded when appropriate. Take this time to simply reflect on the distance you have come. Look back at your lessons and the subjects of the Jedi Circle.

This is why I love ending with the five truths and commitment. What is better than your own experience and progress to show the value?

Closing Thoughts:

This was once a training program offered at the Jedi Academy online website. A way to help those seeking to be and live as Jedi accomplish that goal. For many such a goal is simply impossible, it is laughable. Yet I have never known the word impossible to stop humanity. From space travel to cell phones, from underdog champions to people beating a deadly disease. Time and again humans have found a way to make the impossible a reality.

The Jedi may not get cool looking lightsabers or wear the big comfy robes, yet the ideology is something that is tangible. This is something that can be done, experienced, and results speak for themselves. After a month of living the practices people mention the difference in the way they feel, they way the look at the world, how they approach life. And this directly affects how they interact with the world around.

Jedi may not be saving the galaxy, but we can certainly make a difference in our own worlds. That world, that circle of friends, family, community. We can make a positive and beneficial impact in people's lives. An idea of world-betterment through self-betterment. It is a slow process, it works on a small scale, but it is one that has proven itself viable and doable. If the ideals of the Jedi Circle speak to you then live it. Be a Jedi. Make the word mean something more than Sci-Fi characters.

If you are looking for something you can do daily I offer this. Small little daily exercises you can do which incorporate the Five Practices of the Jedi. Note that these are **not** to replace or be replaced by your current studies and activities. Meaning, if you already do a specific meditation, you are still to practice what is listed here. If you work-out and cover these exercises you are still to do them at some point. These are supplemental exercises for daily use, to be used in conjunction with your current lifestyle.

•**Physical Fitness** - Start with some light stretching (touch the toes, reaching for the sky, etc.). A little knee high marching in place. Now - Do 25 jumping jacks, 15 push-ups (knee push-ups allowed), 25 crunches (or sit-ups), and 15 squats. Daily, once is fine, any time, I recommend morning right when you get out of bed. Doesn't take me more than 5 minutes to complete.

•**Meditation** - I want you to just breathe. This will be your meditation for now. Just take a moment from time to time and just close your eyes and breathe deeply for a few moments. When in the shower, when waiting for something to load, in the morning before starting the morning routine, before bed, etc. Just take a moment and breathe.

•**Awareness** - Take a moment and just take in your surroundings. Above you, behind you, to the sides, below, just look around, note the things you see. To the left a wall with pictures, a smoke detector above me, window in front, beige house across the street. Do this when out for a walk, when you walk into a new room, go to the movies, etc. Do not try to catalog everything, do not take twenty minutes in the doorway looking at everything, just take the moment and note what you can. The things and people around you.

•**Diplomacy** - This one is a bit tough. Lets make it multi-tiered. First, seek to remove tone and listen to what others are actually saying. If asked to do something, but the tone is harsh and demanding, our ego doesn't appreciate that. Instead seek to simply notice what is said, rather focusing how it was said. We may not know why the tone is off, bad day maybe. Second, accept responsibility for your own tone of voice. How you say things does matter, as we are aware. Lastly work on compromise, on finding middle-ground, on seeing all sides of an issue and seeking the fair solution for all involved.

•**Self-Discipline** - This should be obvious. Just actually follow through on these practices daily. Incorporate them and keep them up for as long as you are in this program.

121

Practice these daily, everyday for the your entire time training and living as a Jedi. You will notice a difference, you will see the benefit. These do support how we live, what we do, and material that we write.

Hopefully your journey into the Jedi Path has been and continues to be a fruitful one. If you are looking for interaction and discussion or you have questions or concerns feel free to join us at http://jediacademyonline.com
Be Well.

Made in the USA
San Bernardino, CA
26 August 2015